Instructor's Manual to Accompany

NEWS REPORTING
AND WRITING

Instructor's Manual to Accompany

NEWS REPORTING
AND WRITING
Eighth Edition

The Missouri Group

Brian S. Brooks
George Kennedy
Daryl R. Moen
Don Ranly

School of Journalism
University of Missouri at Columbia

Bedford / St. Martin's
Boston ▪ New York

Manufactured in the United States of America.

9 8 7 6 5
f e d c b a

For information, write: Bedford/St. Martin's, 75 Arlington Street, Boston, MA 02116   (617-399-4000)

ISBN: 0-312-44902-X
EAN: 978-0-312-44902-5

PREFACE

If you were to compare the definition of news values in this and previous editions, you would see how that definition continues to evolve. In part this reflects the way the craft is being practiced, and in part it reflects the direction in which we hope to nudge it.

We have made these and other changes because our textbook is specifically intended to prepare your students for the journalism of the 21st century. This eighth edition of *News Reporting and Writing* is written for the future rather than the past. In it, we introduce beginning students to the concepts, techniques and workplaces they'll encounter at the turn of the millennium and beyond.

Students will learn what new demands they will face as the next generation of journalists. They will learn the skills of reporting and writing necessary to meet those demands. They will learn to use their computers as tools for reporting as well as for writing. They will learn the possibilities and the limitations of online media.

They will also learn that some things—such as the importance of accuracy and fairness, the requirements of clear, compelling writing, and the joy of a story well told—haven't changed and won't change.

In the exercises at the end of each chapter and in the workbook, we have retained the proven features that have been used to teach thousands of students through seven previous editions. We still try to practice what we preach with concrete examples, clear writing and skill-building exercises. We still begin each chapter with a concise explanation of what it is intended to teach. We still stress the fundamentals—thorough reporting, good writing, fair treatment.

As always, we cannot provide answers to every exercise because some of the exercises are open-ended. You and other teachers often localize them. In most cases where there isn't a specific answer, we have tried to identify the key points to look for.

We would like to hear how you use the book, and we encourage feedback on the exercises you have tried that worked or didn't work, as well as suggestions for exercises you assign that aren't in the book or workbook. We would be happy to incorporate your suggestions in future editions. You can reach us at the School of Journalism, University of Missouri, Columbia, Mo. 65211. Or contact us by e-mail. We would be delighted to hear from you.

Brian S. Brooks   *BrooksBS@missouri.edu*
George Kennedy   *KennedyG@missouri.edu*
Daryl R. Moen   *MoenD@missouri.edu*
Don Ranly   *RanlyD@missouri.edu*

CONTENTS

SAMPLE SYLLABUS

News 105

Welcome to News 105 (J105). This course will introduce you to the fundamentals of news judgment, reporting and writing for the first decade of the 21st century and beyond. You also will learn about:

- Professional standards and ethics.
- Cultural awareness.
- Current events and how to keep up with them.
- Associated Press and local *(Missourian)* style rules.
- Using the tools of your trade, including your computer.

We will meet twice a week for two hours each time. In general, the first class of the week will include lectures, discussions and a style quiz. During the second class each week, you may have current events and textbook quizzes, and you may write stories based on lectures and your reading assignments.

You also will have reporting and writing assignments outside of class. Most of these assignments are listed in the syllabus. Because news is frequently unpredictable, other assignments or changes to the syllabus may be made based on news events or the availability of speakers and newsmakers.

Journalists generally must operate on a deadline. You will need to be able to type 40 words per minute with reasonable accuracy. Typing errors are easy to correct on the computer, but you must be able to get your story written quickly.

Journalists also must be reliable. In the profession, missing assignments can cost you your job. Here, if you miss a class, you are likely to miss a graded assignment, which will affect your final grade.

Required Texts

News Reporting and Writing (Brooks, Kennedy, Moen and Ranly)
The Word (Rene J. Cappon)
The Associated Press Stylebook and Libel Manual
J104/105 Manual (available at the university bookstore)
Columbia Missourian (subscription available at the newspaper business office in the *Missourian* lobby)

Recommended Texts

Working with Words (Brooks and Pinson)
Webster's New World Dictionary (paperback college edition is preferable)

Quizzes

Quizzes on current events, the reading assignments and AP style will be given throughout the semester. You will be expected to be familiar with the following:

- People and events in the news locally, nationally and internationally. You must read the *Missourian* every day. Good journalists are

well-informed news consumers; we recommend that you get in the habit of reading a daily metropolitan newspaper and a weekly newsmagazine and of watching daily televised newscasts.
- Newswriting style quizzes are comprehensive, so material covered in early quizzes may be repeated.
- Material covered in assigned readings.

The *AP Stylebook* and local (J104/105) style manual are to be used for all writing assignments. You are responsible for using correct spelling, grammar and usage from the beginning of the semester.

Make-ups: Your instructor will determine whether to allow you to make up work you missed because of an absence. You must talk with your instructor within one week of a missed class to see if make-up work will be permitted. You should have a compelling reason for any absence.

Grading of Writing Assignments

Course grades will be awarded according to the following standards:

A: *Outstanding performance.* Copy usually is publishable with little or no editing.

B: *Superior performance.* Copy usually is publishable with minor editing and revisions.

C: *Adequate performance.* Portions of copy probably would need to be rewritten and closely edited before story could be published.

D: *Marginal performance.* Copy contains major factual, structural, writing and usage flaws. It is doubtful whether it could be published.

F: *Unacceptable performance.* Copy fails to meet even minimum standards for the assignment.

Factual accuracy—including correctly spelled names of people, places, organizations and institutions—is of the utmost importance in your writing. Factual errors will significantly affect your grade. When you graduate, they will affect your job.

Quiz scores also will be an important factor in your final grade.

The scoring of writing assignments, based on points, is designed to take into account improvement over the course of the semester. Assignments toward the end of the semester will count more heavily.

Students must earn at least a C in J105 before they may take any course for which it is a prerequisite.

During the semester, students will work two four-hour shifts at the *Missourian* and two four-hour shifts at radio station KBIA. Students will be at KBIA during the week of Oct. 10 and at the *Missourian* the week of Oct. 24. During the shifts you will act as news observers and analysts and write a report on what constitutes news, how sources are selected and how news reports develop from the initial assignment to the finished product.

The "issue" story at the end of the semester is the final exam for the course.

Grade Changes

If you believe a mistake has been made in a grade, you must see the instructor within one week after the assignment has been returned to you.

J105 Grammar Test

All J105 students must pass a standard grammar test with a score of at least 80 percent before receiving a grade for the course. The grammar test will be given at 5 p.m. Sept. 21 in Gannett Auditorium. The test takes about an hour.

Grammar review sessions and one retake will be arranged if you fail to score 80 percent on the first grammar test. Students who fail to pass the test by the end of the semester will receive an Incomplete grade in this course and will not be able to take any course for which J105 is a prerequisite.

Academic Honesty

Journalists are expected to uphold the highest ethical standards. Any instance of academic dishonesty will be reported to the provost's office.

Academic dishonesty includes, but is not limited to, the following:

- Plagiarism (copying work written or published by others).
- Inappropriate eye movements.
- Looking at or copying another student's work, or allowing another student to look at or copy your work.
- Talking or otherwise communicating with another student during quizzes or writing assignments, unless instructed to do so.
- Removing test materials or attempting to remove them from an examination room.

These rules apply to all quizzes, as well as to both in-class and outside-class assignments.

Failure to meet these standards will result in zero points for the quiz or writing assignment. You will also risk failing the course.

Schedule of Classes

Week	First Session	Second Session	Outside
1		Introduction to news	
2	Introduction to computers	Developing news judgment	
3	Characteristics of newswriting (personality profiles introduced)	Writing inverted pyramid leads	
4	Determining news values for press releases	News stories based on press releases	
5	Obituary as a news story	Obituaries	Profile ideas due; grammar test
6	Databases	Databases	
7	Interviewing and personality profiles (issue story introduced)	Student profiles (out of class)	

Week	First Session	Second Session	Outside
8	Ethics, sensitivity discussion (issue story introduced)	Midterm exam	
9	Covering public meetings	Write city council story (in class)	Radio report due
10	Broadcast news	Reporting with numbers	Profile (first draft) due
11	Speeches as news stories	Write speech story (in class)	*Missourian* report due
12	Humanized news writing	Write humanized obit	Cover council meeting; story due noon the next day. Issue idea due
13	Accidents, crimes	Write accident story	Revision of profile due
14	Instructor's choice	Thanksgiving	
15	Follow stories	Write follow story	Speech story due
16	Instructor's choice	Instructor's choice	Issue story due

Schedule of Style Quizzes

Week	Quiz Topic
3	Common stylebook rules (from your manual)
4	*Missourian* local style (from your manual)
5	Grammar, spelling and usage (from appendix, *News Reporting and Writing*)
6	Punctuation and hyphenation (from text appendix)
7	Capitalization (from appendix)
8	Abbreviations and acronyms (from appendix)
9	Numerals (from appendix)

Reading Assignments

Reading assignments are from *News Reporting and Writing, The Word* and the J104/J105 manual. After the first week, students are expected to complete reading assignments by the first class period of the week listed.

Week	Assignment	
1	*News Reporting:*	Chapter 1, The Nature of News
		Chapter 2, The Changing News Business
2	*News Reporting:*	Chapter 7, The Inverted Pyramid
		Chapter 8, Writing to Be Read
	The Word:	Chapter 1, Language
		Chapter 2, News Writing
		Chapter 3, Leads

PART ONE: JOURNALISM AND JOURNALISTS

CHAPTER 1: THE NATURE OF NEWS

Overview

The forward-looking orientation of this book begins at the beginning, with the opening scene. Like most of the illustrations in the book, this one is taken from life. News room visits and conversations with planners from Raleigh, N.C., to Portland, Ore., keep the authors—and your students—in touch with the rapidly changing realities of journalism at the turn of the millennium.

We show, rather than just tell, about-to-be journalists and consumers of journalism how practices and news values are evolving. Beginning in this chapter and continuing throughout the book, we stress what the professionals stress: the central importance of relevance, usefulness and interest. We also emphasize, as the professionals do, the unchanging importance of accuracy, fairness and serving the needs of your audience.

A few words about the exercises. Those of you who are experienced instructors may well prefer to substitute your own exercises and local examples for those we provide. So much the better. We seek to provide you and your students with realism, variety and the opportunity to apply textbook lessons to real-life situations. This edition includes, in every chapter, opportunities for students to use the computer as a reporting tool. Every chapter also provides at least one "challenge" exercise intended to stretch the abilities of your best students.

Solutions to Textbook Questions and Exercises

1. This exercise has the potential for a week's or a term's worth of discussion. Indeed, the principles and applications you explore here will—and should—recur throughout the course. Obviously, there are no right or wrong answers. The point is to get the students to think about the real-world uses of the criteria outlined in the chapter. There'll be grist here for argument, both among class members and with the judgments of the editors. Your students may well discover that not all editors apply the criteria in the same ways. They may discover news judgments that are inexplicable using only these criteria. Fair enough. Perhaps the most important lesson to come from this exercise may be that journalism is still much more an art than a science, with many more guidelines than hard-and-fast rules.

2. The differences may be even more striking than with a similar analysis of your local newspaper. For years, the *Times* was highly conservative in news judgments, as in design and writing. The paper has changed more than most over a generation. Still, it remains the standard against which most American journalists measure other newspapers and other news judgments.

3. Many instructors already have developed close working relationships with local professionals, of course. Few of your students will ever have had this chance, however. Most professionals will welcome such opportunities.

4. Of course, the choice of frame will depend on the subject and the writer. The importance of this exercise is less in which frame is chosen than in the reasoning process and consideration of the implications of the choice. A public or civic journalism frame will be one that puts the interest of the citizens ahead of any other. A story told in a civic journalism frame will include the information a citizen needs in order to act.
5. This exercise, of course, assumes access to the Internet. The array of bulletin boards, special-interest groups and news-and-information providers should enable students to find the requested sources and consumer material without much trouble. (For suggestions, you may wish to skip ahead to Chapter 5, Gathering Information, which offers how-to guidance for online reporting.)

Solutions to Workbook Questions and Exercises

1. If the editors of the campus and community papers are applying the criteria for news judgment to their different audiences, there should be little overlap in the papers' content. Even campus news, which you'd expect to find in the community paper of a college town, probably will be written and presented with different perspectives (and, often, different language).

   Unless your students are long-time residents of the community, they'll probably find the campus paper's content more relevant, useful and interesting. It may be interesting to compare your perspective to theirs.

   Differences in audience should be obvious. Students probably care little about local politics, tax rates or the condition of the public schools. Readers of the community paper, who probably tend to be long-time residents, care about all three. The townsfolk, conversely, are likely to be less interested in rock music, student politics or the inadequacies of student advising.
2. Students probably will notice many of the same topics reported in print and on television, but the reporting will be noticeably different. Pictures are essential to television. Therefore, fires, accidents and festivals are more likely to be defined as important news. City council meetings typically make dull video, however important the discussion topics. So the council meeting is much more likely to be the newspaper's lead story than it is to be at the top of the television report. Details, statistics, box scores, obituaries—all are common in the newspaper and missing from television.

   Students should also notice that, largely because of the central importance of the video image, television and newspaper journalists apply the same criteria in quite different ways. Look for attempts to use the emotional impact of pictures, whether for tragedy or farce. Look for the dramatizing of conflict. Look for the emphasis on timeliness, especially in "live" reports—even if what's being shown isn't very important by the traditional criteria.
3. The wire services, of course, supply far more national and international news than most local papers or stations can use or want to use. "Localness" is an implicit news value that is becoming more important as the range of sources for nonlocal information multiplies. Students might look

especially for attempts to find local angles or connections to news from distant points.

4. The biggest difference, of course, is the amount of material available online compared to any edition of any newspaper or any newscast. Your local paper and stations will have their own Web sites, usually with links to other information. The national sites are likely to be updated more often and to have information that isn't in print or on the air. Most students are likely to be more familiar with and comfortable with online sources.

5. a. Encourage your students to pay special attention to the differences in emphasis between the local and national papers. If *USA Today* circulates in your area, it may be possible to learn whether it has had any impact on the design or content of the local paper.

   b. Obviously, *USA Today* looks for stories with national appeal. It publishes more and shorter stories than do most papers, with considerable emphasis on social and economic issues. The editors try to strike a local chord with brief state-by-state roundups of items.

6. This exercise serves at least two purposes: First, it requires practical application of the criteria discussed in the chapter; second, it forces students to look closely at the community in which they are living. The story ideas will vary widely. What matters is that students are able to justify their work in terms of the criteria for news judgment.

7. A. a. The police chief as man of the year, of course, involves mainly prominence, with proximity a factor.

      b. The story of the arrested employee is unusual. There also are elements of conflict and proximity.

      c. The problems of the cancer detection center will have impact, as well as conflict and proximity.

   B. The story of the cancer detection center has the greatest news value because of its impact. The man of the year story is probably least significant.

8. a. The library sources should include newspaper and magazine articles on both the issues and the speakers. *The New York Times Index, Facts on File* and the *Congressional Quarterly's* Weekly Report are good places to start. You can look ahead to the sources of information listed in Chapters 2 and 5 for other suggestions, including sources available in computer databases.

   b. The local newspaper is a good place to start. A spokesperson for the American Civil Liberties Union is sure to raise constitutional questions. Check with experts from the nearest medical school and law school. On the pro-testing side may be local employers and law enforcement agencies. The guidelines in the chapter will be useful in evaluating all these sources.

9. a.-b. Follow the same procedures as in exercise 8.

10. In the real case from which this exercise is drawn, the decision was not to publish. The rationale was that the extent of the nurse's culpability for the death was unclear and that the mere publication of her name would inevitably suggest guilt. Arguments for publishing include the following: Names add credibility to a story. Circumstantial evidence strongly suggests

3

that the nurse is either being disciplined or being made a scapegoat, both newsworthy developments.

11. The obvious benefits are the verification of both detail and context before publication (as opposed to waiting for complaints after publication), together with the protections that verified accuracy offers. There also is a public relations benefit with both sources and readers. Possible drawbacks are the opportunity provided for sources to withdraw controversial quotes or to try to edit stories. You and your students may think of other pluses or minuses.

12. **CHALLENGE EXERCISE.**   This should be an enlightening, though time-consuming, exercise. If your accuracy check turns up any complaints of inaccuracy or unfairness, you may want to add a step—a response from the newspaper. Warning: Many newspaper editors are hypersensitive to the kind of critical scrutiny they insist on for others. You may strike some sparks.

CHAPTER 2: THE CHANGING NEWS BUSINESS

Overview

This chapter has been extensively rewritten to acquaint students with the significant changes taking place in the news business. In particular, it highlights the emergence of convergence efforts across the country. As before, the chapter describes the typical organization of news rooms, the roles of editors and potential jobs in each medium.

Solutions to Textbook Questions and Exercises

1. This exercise is designed to get students to think about how a newspaper is organized. It is much more effective to have students create their own charts than to have them memorize or explain standard organizational charts. In the process of doing the exercise, they will be forced to talk with staff members about the organization of the newspaper.

2. The same is true of this exercise. Students gain a better understanding of the copy flow process if they chart it themselves. Because the process is different at almost every newspaper, we have not provided a standard chart other than the one in the text.

3. This duplicates exercise 1 but at a television station rather than at a newspaper. Make sure that students show the relationship between the reporter, videographer, producer and news director.

4. Finding census data on the Internet is easy. Just go to the U.S. Census Bureau's World Wide Web site (http://www.census.gov) and start searching. You'll find answers to all the questions at that site.

5. No definitive answer to this question can be provided here. Each of these services regularly adds and drops news sources. The exercise is designed to make students aware of the news material available on such services.

6. There are many sources of information on the Internet, which is arguably the world's largest library. As a result, the possibilities are endless. Note, however, that federal government resources alone make the Internet an indispensable source of information for reporters.

1. This exercise is designed to show students the incredible depth of computer-based media compared with television or even newspapers. Of course, this is an open-ended exercise, so we can provide no solution here. However, look for an understanding on students' part of the increased depth of computer-based media. Also, look for an acknowledgment that students find the computer-based media much easier to search.

2. This exercise is designed to do many of the same things as exercise 1. However, if access to one of the commercial databases is a financial problem, using the World Wide Web, easily accessible on most college and university campuses, may be preferable. Excellent college newspaper sites are found at Kansas State University (http://www.kstatecollegian.com) and the University of California at Berkeley (http://www.dailycal.org).

3. Information on public trading among newspaper companies can be found in various places where quarterly reports are posted. CompuServe is an excellent place to search. If your students need advice on which companies to include, suggest Gannett, Knight-Ridder, Times Mirror, Scripps-Howard, the Tribune Co. and the New York Times Co. Gannett owns the most newspapers.

4. AOL Time Warner owns, among other things, the magazines *Time, Sports Illustrated, People* and *Money,* as well as Time-Life Music and Time Books. A complete listing of AOL Time Warner properties can be found in the company's quarterly reports, available in many places online. Also check the company's World Wide Web site (http://www.timewarner.com).

5. a. The editor is the top-ranking news executive. He or she is in charge of the news department.
   b. The managing editor is the top-ranking news executive with whom reporters are likely to have frequent contact. The managing editor prepares the news room budget and supervises day-to-day news-gathering operations.
   c. The city editor is in charge of local news coverage. He or she supervises the local reporting staff.
   d. The sports editor supervises all sports coverage for the newspaper. The sports department usually operates its own copy desk operation and reporting staff.
   e. The lifestyle editor supervises the features' section of the newspaper. The lifestyle section is an outgrowth of the old women's sections, but modern lifestyle coverage is much broader in scope. Trends in modern living are reported here.
   f. The news editor usually is in charge of the copy desk operation, although some newspapers refer to their city editors as news editors. At smaller papers, the news editor may function as copy desk chief, but at larger newspapers, those positions are separate.
   g. The state editor, as the title implies, is responsible for state news coverage. If the newspaper's coverage area encompasses more than one state, the state editor may be in charge of wider coverage. State desks usually have reporting staffs and their own copy desk operations.
   h. The editorial page editor is in charge of day-to-day supervision of editorial page content. He or she reports directly to the editor, who may

be expected to approve all editorials before publication. Typically, the editorial page editor is the only page or section editor who reports directly to the editor.

   i. The graphics editor is in charge of all maps, charts and other graphic devices that appear in a newspaper. This may include both locally produced and syndicated graphics material. In some cases, the graphics editor and the photo editor work in close coordination.

   j. The copy desk chief is responsible for the smooth operation of the main copy desk. Often, the desk chief actually does the page layout for the front page of the paper. The desk chief also coordinates the various desks responsible for page design.

6. a. The advertising department produces most of the revenue of the typical U.S. newspaper. It usually is divided into classified and display ad departments. Larger newspapers may also have separate national advertising and advertising art departments.

   b. The circulation department is responsible for distribution of the newspaper. This involves coordination of the various bundle haulers, youth carriers and motor-route carriers. The circulation manager is also responsible for supervision of the mail room, where various sections of the paper are assembled and bundled for distribution.

   c. The business department is responsible for billing, accounting and related functions. Employee relations falls under this department, so matters such as negotiations with company unions also fall under the aegis of the business department. The newspaper's general manager usually has direct responsibility for this department.

   d. The production department is responsible for actually assembling the creative work of the news and advertising departments and for producing the finished product. The composing room, camera room and press room fall under the supervision of the production manager or production superintendent.

7. a. The news director is in charge of all news operations at a broadcast station. His or her newspaper equivalent would be the editor.

   b. The newsanchor is the on-air personality who leads the viewer through the newscast. He or she reads news stories and introduces the accounts of reporters.

   c. The news producer is in charge of the overall flow of the news show. The producer makes certain that videotapes and graphics are cued on time and in the proper order.

   d. A videographer is a television news camera operator.

   e. A reporter is one who reports a news story from the scene of an event or in the studio.

8. If a college magazine is examined, answers to this question will vary depending on the organization in place on your campus. However, in most cases the following descriptions would apply:

   a. The editor is in charge of all editorial operations of the magazine.

   b. The art director is usually in charge of producing both photographs and graphics and may supervise several photographers or artists.

9. There are as many organizational structures at broadcast stations and newspapers as there are broadcast stations and newspapers. The purpose of this exercise is not to depict a typical organization but to make the stu-

dent think about how media operations are organized. Visiting a station or newspaper for this assignment will force students to talk to people about what they do. In the process, the organizational structure should become clear.

10. In any organization with well-educated people, there are likely to be personality clashes that lead to the politicization of the workplace atmosphere. Newspapers are not immune to this problem. A good way to introduce this topic to students is to offer hypothetical situations that lead to further discussion. Here are some examples:

    a. The managing editor has hired his son, an English literature major at an exclusive university, as a summer intern. In the process of doing so, he bypassed several top students from the area's best journalism program. This has created animosity on the part of the editors who must work with the managing editor's son. They resent the son's presence and have made him feel uncomfortable. Because your desk is next to his, you are caught between your editors and the managing editor's son, all of whom have discussed the situation with you. You are a new reporter with less than a year on the job. How do you deal with the situation?

    b. You have joined the staff of a large newspaper in the middle of a dispute over whether the news room should be organized by the Newspaper Guild, the labor union that represents reporters in more than 100 cities. You are asked to rally behind the union cause. Doing so may well alienate you from the editors who hired you. Failure to do so may estrange you from your co-workers. How do you respond?

11. **CHALLENGE EXERCISE.** It is extremely important for a new reporter to adjust quickly to the job. First impressions on the part of editors often are lasting. A good way to approach this topic is to ask students to describe how they would go about winning the confidence of their editors. The exercise is designed to encourage students to think about how they will approach the critical process of adjusting to the job.

12. **CHALLENGE EXERCISE.** Students should be able to find the following information: Clint Eastwood was born in San Francisco on May 31, 1930. He has directed several movies and performed in many. He is best-known for his roles in *Dirty Harry, In the Line of Fire, Unforgiven, A Fistful of Dollars, Pale Rider* and *The Bridges of Madison County*. A more complete biography can be obtained from the actors' database in Lexis/Nexis.

PART TWO: REPORTING TOOLS

CHAPTER 3: INTERVIEWING

Overview

The importance of interviewing cannot be overstated. It is the crux of the news-gathering operation. What often differentiates the good reporter from the average one is not only the ability to ask the right questions but also the knowledge of how to ask them.

In this chapter, students will learn how to prepare for the interview and several ways to conduct one. You should emphasize to students that there is no one correct way to conduct interviews. The methods they use depend on the person being interviewed, the type of information sought and the time they have to get it. There is a difference between interviewing someone about an honor just received and interviewing a public official about possible malfeasance, but it is possible to get the necessary information in both instances.

Students can learn the techniques of interviewing by reading this chapter and the related readings, but they cannot learn how to interview unless they actually do it. That is why it is so important for the instructor to assign as much interviewing as time will permit. If the circumstances do not allow you to send students into the community for interviews, we urge you to set up role-playing situations in class. You may want to begin by playing either yourself or someone in the news, such as your state's senior senator. You can prepare yourself by reading the memos prepared by the students. After you have played the senator, let students play the parts of both the reporter and the person being interviewed. Ask the class to comment on the techniques and the questions asked or not asked.

Solutions to Textbook Questions and Exercises

1. The students should be using *Who's Who*, the *Readers' Guide to Periodical Literature* and clips from the newspaper library. If your students have access to electronic database searches, this exercise will provide valuable practice in this area. To illustrate the value of the searches, you could have the class discuss and prepare a list of qualifications to narrow the search and then have one person bring the list of stories back to the class. Or, you might arrange for a librarian to meet with the class to talk about how the database searches could be conducted. If you do not have database access, try taking your students to the library or the offices of the local newspaper to conduct the searches.
2. Open-ended questions are worded to permit a range of responses.
3. Closed-ended questions narrow the possible responses.
4. The experience of being interviewed is an essential part of your class. Few reporters have ever been interviewed. It is important that all journalists learn what it is like to be on the other end of the questions. They should experience the helplessness of not being in control of the interview, of not choosing what gets in and what does not, and they should see how many

mistakes—both of fact and of context—are made by the reporter. This gives students more respect for the problems involved in interviewing. We turn the stories over to the student who is the subject of the interview and have that student indicate all errors of fact and context and write a comment about how the interview was conducted. Did the interviewer put me at ease, listen closely to my responses, ask obvious follow-up questions? Then we look at the stories and add our comments. Only then are the stories returned to the writer. If you can use only one exercise in this chapter, please use this one.

5. This exercise gives you an opportunity to localize the exercises as much as you wish. If you use this question, you may wish to identify students who will be working on the same subject individually. That gives you an opportunity to compare the responses.

Solutions to Workbook Questions and Exercises

1. For those people with national and international reputations, students should be using Internet sources, *Who's Who*, the *Readers' Guide to Periodical Literature* and clips from the newspaper library. If you do not have access to a clip library, arrange to copy the clips from your local newspaper's library and distribute them to the class.

   The memo should test the same things the inverted pyramid does: The student must select those things pertinent to the assignment. Feel free to change the focus of any of the exercises. Make them as timely as possible.

2. Here are questions that you could ask your state's governor about higher education.

   a. *Open-ended questions:*
      1. What role does higher education play in the political process?
      2. How could the leaders of higher education be more effective in representing their cause?
      3. What is your assessment of higher education in this state?
      4. What role, if any, should the governor play in promoting higher education's interests?
      5. Assess the legislature's successes and failures on higher education issues so far in your term.

   b. *Closed-ended questions:* (Instructors: Note that these questions should be much more specific to your governor and should be based on the research the students have done about the issues.)
      1. How have you improved higher education in this state?
      2. Could the leaders of the higher education institutions in this state spend their money more wisely than they are doing?
      3. In public, almost everyone is for higher education. Are there any powerful interests or individuals who privately argue against more money for higher education?
      4. At this moment, what other issues in this state take precedence over higher education?
      5. Have the leaders of the higher education system in this state been effective spokespeople?

9

3. a. *Open-ended questions:*
   1. This is a big operation. How do you keep track of the finances of this agency?
   2. If someone in this agency were embezzling money, how would the system catch him or her?
   3. Would you talk about the responsibilities you have in your role as administrator of this agency?
   b. *Closed-ended questions:*
   1. Is your salary commensurate with your responsibilities?
   2. What fringe benefits do you get?
   3. Are the de facto rules governing checks written to you any different from those for the other employees? (Instructors: Obviously, if a reporter had evidence of embezzlement, he or she would eventually draw the noose tighter and present the evidence. The questions eventually would come to the point that the reporter is asking: "How do you explain check No. 101 written to you with no documentation in the files?")
   c. The open-ended questions are the least threatening. They also produce less information. They are, however, helpful in getting the source on record on some issues before you move on to specifics.
4. The questions should go from the general to the specific. The reporter is searching for a focus. As soon as that focus is identified, then the questions should probably be mostly closed-ended.
   1. Which of your accomplishments do you think were most important in your winning the scholarship?
   2. Who are the people most responsible for helping you prepare to win this honor?
   3. Did you talk to any previous winners of this award? If so, what did you learn from them?
   4. Describe your reaction to hearing the news.
   5. What are your career goals?
   6. What will you study abroad?
   7. How will this year as a Rhodes Scholar help you achieve your career goals?
   8. What advice do you have for others who may be thinking of applying for this scholarship?
5. 1. What are the pros and cons of having dedicated scholarship money for minorities?
   2. What have you heard from people in your constituency representing either side of the issue?
   3. How did you arrive at your position on the issue?
   4. If you were voting on a recommendation to the university to cut off all scholarship money dedicated to minorities, how would you vote?
6. a. The point here is that almost without exception, there will be no rapport established on camera. There is too little time. Usually, the on-camera interviewer doesn't even see the source until it is time for the interview. The questions have been written by staff members. Still, on the morning shows, there are some instances when the interviewer will make comments to try to make the source feel relaxed.

b. Students will probably know or can find out something about a person who appeared on a national news show. They can base their answers on backgrounding from newspaper stories or articles tracked down in the *Readers' Guide to Periodical Literature*.

7. First, gather background information. In addition to biographical material, talk to other students to find out what the instructor is like in and out of class. Talk to his or her colleagues to get some insights. When you arrive, you can establish rapport by talking about the instructor's interests in a hobby, children, and so on.

8. It helps students to put their approaches into categories, to understand what they did: "I established rapport this way because of information I obtained before the interview; because of things I spotted in the source's office that I talked about; because I was making small talk and he or she said something that I pursued."

9. Answers will vary. Be sure to collect both the original and the corrected versions.

10. In fact, you might have the students choose a story with multiple sources and have them call or send questionnaires to each of the sources. Or you could choose stories from the local daily. Either way, the purpose is to get students to talk to sources and to see if students can differentiate between legitimate comments and criticisms that are unfair or merely reflect the source's bias.

11. In effect, you are asking the journalist to give you a couple of anecdotes. Besides the lessons students learn by listening to someone else's experiences, they also can show how they handle an anecdote in a story.

12. We urge you to set a standard of accuracy for the class that maintains that a quote is not accurate unless ALL the words are the same and in the correct order. The Associated Press and United Press International stylebooks permit the reporter to correct grammar errors if they are occasional—a slip of speech. If there is a news conference on television, have your reporters cover it. Compare the quotes in their reports to those in papers. You can even have them compare the quotes found in the several versions that are available to them in newspapers.

13. This is another effort to impress on students how difficult it is to be accurate. Too many reporters we send into the profession have the idea that they are accurate when they are not. Reporters need to see how many mistakes they make. Then, perhaps, they will work harder to achieve the standards they think they are setting.

14. The exercise works better if you get the transcript of a press conference because the comments are spontaneous. If the reporters didn't have time to wait for a transcript, students will find that the quotes are not the same in all versions. That will be a springboard to a discussion of accuracy and the importance of taking good notes, perhaps even using tape recorders.

15. The editor will look over the notes. If there are many sentence fragments that turned up as full quotes or if there are sentences with words left out that the reporter filled in later, then the editor should suspect that the reporter may not be accurate. If the reporter has gone through a few exercises, such as the one in 14, then he or she will recognize that mistakes are possible.

16. a. Registrar, recruiting officer, cross section of students.
    b. State and local figures, source of study, comparable figures from previous school years.
    c. Answers will vary.
17. **CHALLENGE EXERCISE.**   Of course, there are several different angles that could be emphasized in writing the story. Which one the writer chooses depends on the news values of the publication and what is currently of public interest. The following version assumes that the four problem areas are of equal importance. In a real situation, any one of the four may be worth emphasizing. For instance, if the university was still having major problems in minority recruitment, it might be appropriate to lead with the chancellor's comments on that subject.

> In an interview one week after resigning as chancellor of Springfield University, Barbara Behling said she had corrected four major problem areas during her eight years in office.
> Behling, attracted from Oklahoma by a search committee indicating the Springfield campus was ready for change, identified the four areas as the University hospital, the disrepair of the campus, the structure of the campus administration and minority recruitment.
> The hospital was the major problem.
> "The legislature was concerned about hospital financing," she said. "The place looked bad. There was no stopping and thinking about whether I had to do something; it had to be done."
> When she left the campus, the hospital's budget had risen from $50 million to $125 million while the state's contribution declined from about 33 percent to 15 percent.
> Soon after she arrived, she received a proposal to build a new law school. The questions she asked, she said, made her realize how much planning had to be done before the physical plant could be improved.
> She took three steps: She hired a consultant to suggest short-term projects. She wanted them, she said, "to make the campus look better and make people feel better about it."
> She ordered good documentation on campus maintenance and then began long-term planning. There is now about $145 million worth of construction completed or in process on projects that came out of the long-range plan.

If this structure were continued, the story would go on to report her work on the two remaining problem areas in the same order in which they were introduced.

From the information given to the student, one possibility for an ending would be this quote: "I had a lot to learn in a short time about the institution. I had to do a lot of listening."

However, the answers to follow-up questions would probably reveal more personal and insightful information.

What this edited version of the interview lacks is any real questions getting at Behling's feelings, her emotions. The interviewer does not press her to evaluate her performance; she merely recites the accomplishments.

CHAPTER 4: IN THEIR OWN WORDS

Overview

Knowing how and when to quote is an essential skill for any reporter; knowing how and when to attribute sources is equally important. We believe the subjects are important enough for a separate chapter.

You may wish to begin a discussion about quotations by reviewing the basic rules of using quotation marks. Note the box in the text that demonstrates the correct use and placement of quotation marks.

Students may not know how to handle quoted material inside quotations. Or they may not know how to punctuate a continuing quotation, as in the following:

> "The first word of a continuing sentence," the professor said, "is never capitalized after the attribution."

A mistake students often make is to close the quotation at the end of a paragraph, even though the same speaker is quoted at the beginning of the next paragraph. The wire service style rules for punctuation in quotations are found in the "quotation marks" and "comma" entries of the stylebooks.

After you are sure that students understand basic punctuation rules, you can stress the importance of using quotes and recording them accurately. However, it is our belief that beginning reporters often use quotes only because they have recorded them accurately. You can find examples of this in any newspaper, and it would be good to analyze them with the class. We suggest using transparencies and an overhead projector. Point out examples of quotes that should have been paraphrased or perhaps not used at all.

In the section on attribution, perhaps what you need to stress most is the use of the word "say." English instructors probably will have urged students to use synonyms for "say," but most editors prefer to avoid those synonyms. Stress the importance of attribution, but keep the students from including attribution two or three times per paragraph, even if the source is the same.

In the section on correcting quotes, we included a discussion of the widely differing views and practices. In doing so, we hope to prepare students for the real world and to stress the importance of knowing a publication's policy. This is even more crucial for students concentrating on magazine journalism or public relations. For the record, however, we make our position clear: Without question, you should know the policy of your news organization regarding the use of direct quotations. But equally without question, that policy should be that you place inside quotation marks only the exact words of the speaker. Make that your personal policy, and you can't go wrong.

In the section concerning on- and off-the-record information, you can see immediately that there is no agreement on the concepts of *off-the-record, not for attribution, background* and *deep background*. The most important points in this section are the following: "Your obligation is to make sure that you and your sources understand each other. Set the ground rules ahead of time. Clarify your terms. And be sure you know the policy of your paper in these matters."

1. This concise exercise deals with some of the key problems with direct quotations discussed in the text. No two people will agree on every decision to be made here, but some are obvious. Discussing students' decisions in class is most worthwhile. For example, rather than quote the young man directly, it is sufficient to mention that he speaks slowly and in incomplete sentences. Probably we do not want Mrs. O'Reilly calling the doctors "hacks" or the prison officials "vicious." Here's one way to rewrite the story. Note that the attributions are in the present tense.

> Christopher O'Reilly is a remarkably happy young man, despite a bout with meningitis eight years ago that has left him paralyzed and brain-damaged.
>
> He has much to be happy about. Physical therapy has hastened his recovery since the day he awoke from a 10-week-long coma. He has lived to celebrate his 26th birthday.
>
> He speaks slowly about his birthday party, celebrated with friends and a big cake.
>
> He lives in a house with his mother and stepfather in the rolling, green countryside near Springfield.
>
> His mother talks about the sad condition he was in when he came out of his coma. Doctors predicted that he would remain a vegetable all his life. "He couldn't talk; he could only blink," she says.
>
> Now, Chris is able to respond in incomplete sentences to questions and can carry on a slow communication. His mother says he doesn't talk well, "but he talks."
>
> It all began when he stole a neighbor's Rototiller. His probation was revoked, and he found himself in the medium-security prison in Springfield. Then came what the O'Reilly family called "inadequate medical treatment" in the prison system. The family argued that he received punishment beyond what the Eighth Amendment of the U.S. Constitution calls cruel and unusual.
>
> As a result, he was awarded $250,000 from the state, the largest legal settlement in federal court in 10 years.
>
> "That sounds like a lot of money," his mother says. "But it really isn't, you know, when you consider what happened and when you consider the worth of a human life." She says the state should have paid at least a million dollars.
>
> O'Reilly contracted the infection of the brain after sleeping on the concrete floor of a confinement cell, his mother says. He had been placed in solitary confinement because he would not clean his cell. The disease went undiagnosed for eight days and left him paralyzed and brain-damaged, she says.

2. You may wish to have the students assume they are covering this speech for the local paper. The importance of the exercise, however, is to have students discuss the merits of the various quotes. Are they unique or phrased uniquely? Are they important words by an important person?
   As examples, here are some striking quotes:

- "Your ability to motivate others is, according to the research, dependent *mostly* upon your credibility."
- "... the most important and first component of credibility is good, old-fashioned *sociability*."
- "There is no substitute for knowledge."

3. Getting quotations down correctly is a skill that needs lots of practice. If students use a digital tape recorder, they can note the spot on the tape and find the quote easily. If you send the whole class or several members to the same speech or meeting, you can also compare the lines that students thought significant enough to quote directly.
4. This exercise may be disconcerting to journalism students because they are likely to find that some reporters have not given much thought to these questions. The results will make for good class discussion.
5. Your school library probably has some computer database to which students have access. Students may be surprised how much has been written on this subject.
6. You may wish to do this as an in-class exercise. The story need not be a long one. Ask students to read their quotes aloud to see the reaction of the person quoted. Students are often surprised by what reporters choose to quote and how their words are used or abused.

Solutions to Workbook Questions and Exercises

1. There is no way to give one correct version of these sentences. Students will rewrite them in different ways. The benefit of the exercise will come from the discussion. If a student has elected to paraphrase a direct quote, he or she should have a good reason for doing so. Following are suggested ways to handle the quotations.
   a. The group will be recording this spring, says John Dade, guitarist, singer and songwriter, who first began singing with Don Seiver about three years ago. "There will be a product on the streets—on the airwaves, we hope—by the end of the summer."
   b. The group performed with Taylor Brown and John Barnes last summer in New York, Dade says. "John has been a fan for a while and Taylor turned into a real solid supporter."
   c. "It took me a long time to shuck the robe of responsibility," recalls Seiver. Although he loved writing songs and playing guitar, for three years he struggled over whether he could make a living at it. He thought he had to be an English teacher just in case. (The rest of the quotation makes little sense.)
   d. Nobody settles for anything less than the best, Dade said. The group squabbles about the fine points, but the creative tension builds as the group molds a new song.
   e. (Leave as is.)
   f. "It makes it more real," says Seiver. "It makes it feel like you're living. When I'm on the road, I'm always staying with friends. Traveling can really get you down."
   g. (Leave as is, including the "ain't.")

15

h. Says Dade: "You don't have to live in Hollywood Hills. You don't have to drive a Mercedes-Benz. You don't have to hang out at the Rainbow Club."

2. In the second paragraph, the quote from the eyewitness should be edited. For example:

> One eyewitness said: "I saw the plane coming lower and lower. I knew it would never make it to the airport."

There is no need to quote the unnamed official who said, "We'll look into this thoroughly."
Keep the quote from Marvin Anderson.
The quote from Curtis Vokamer is excellent and should be kept.
Also keep the quotation from the United spokesperson.
The quotation from Alderman James Staley is a troublesome one. Journalists do not agree on how this type of quote should be handled. An easy way out would be to drop the quote altogether. Most journalists would at least get rid of the "da" and the "gonna."
The quote of the eyewitness regarding the cocktails is potentially libelous and should be dropped.
Strike the last quote.

3. a. "It's the American dream," Bill Buchanan says.
"There were some hard times I wouldn't want to repeat," says his wife JoAnne. "It was scary at first."
They are talking about owning their own business, a unique relationship that casts husband and wife in the roles of co-bosses.
The marriage survival rate and the small-business survival rate are bad. Trying to put the two together seems like asking for trouble.
However, John Pettey says putting the two together has made marriage and work easier. "It brings us closer together." Pettey and his wife own Pettey's Fashion Cleaners and Laundry, a business they have worked in together for eight years.
"It's great," Pettey says in a slow Southern drawl. "She does the books and I do all the work in the back. It's easy."
"It was unreal at the beginning," Mrs. Buchanan says in contrast. "The time we had to put in so we wouldn't have to hire someone else! We were open 9 to 9 and someone in the family had to be there all the time. It was really a strain on our family at the beginning. But the children were old enough to learn by it, and it added to their education."
The Buchanans own Athlete's Feet, a store specializing in sports clothes. "They (athletic shoes) really took off as a fashion item. If they hadn't, we would have folded," Buchanan says.
Things are running smoothly, so to speak, in the athletic shoe business now, and the Buchanans enjoy it. They started the business eight and a half years ago to have extra income to send their three children to college.
Buchanan likes sports and wanted to open a sporting goods store. He works at Monsanto, working at the store in the afternoons and on Saturdays. He does inventory chores at home in the evenings.

Mrs. Buchanan works from 10 a.m. to 2 p.m. in the store, then does out-of-store errands.

"She manages the store and takes care of writing checks, making orders, keeping books," Buchanan says. "I decide what to order, what styles of shoes and how many. JoAnne, of course, advises me, particularly in tennis clothes, socks, warm-up suits."

Mrs. Buchanan says it's helpful to separate duties. "You can devote time to special duties and not have to worry about the whole thing."

Doug and Patti Lambert own Patti's, a gift shop that began as a plant shop and gradually expanded. They say a division of labor such as the Buchanans have is essential to making a husband-wife business work.

"We have to separate duties because we take everything so seriously," Lambert says. "We fight about where to display something, even if it's only six feet apart."

"Violently," Mrs. Lambert adds, smiling. "There's a lot of stress we wouldn't have if it was just boss to employee. I'd just say, 'Put this here.' As co-bosses, we argue frequently.

"The biggest drawback is taking it home," Mrs. Lambert says. "It's our breakfast and dinner conversation."

Still, having different opinions can help the business in the long run, according to Mrs. Lambert.

"We have different tastes. We like different colors, textures. Doug's very formal; I'm very casual. It gives us more mass appeal."

Lambert adds: "And makes it impossible to get along. It takes an extremely strong marriage to survive it, unless one is subservient—one is boss, the other is servant.

"But we're doing fine."

b. He had to face up to it. He had decided that if he did not run for office, he had no right to complain about the government. "So I ran, and by accident, I won!"

That was in 1988, when T. M. "Bob" Doran, president of Doranco, a drilling contractor in Hobbs, New Mexico, was elected to his first two-year term in the state legislature, the first Republican from his district.

That was 10 years ago, and he has won five elections since then. "I do not really think of myself as a politician and do not have any real ambition of going further in politics," Bob says. "But I feel like now I have the right to complain about things."

Bob had been in the drilling business 13 years when he was elected state representative. But just because he won an election, Bob was not about to leave the oilpatch.

He started working the oilfield when he was 16, and through high school and college he had a variety of jobs in the patch. In 1973, he graduated from Notre Dame with a degree in mechanical engineering.

In 1978, Doranco was started with two power rigs. "We drilled 16 holes that first year. Things were pretty slow until about 1980, when we bought another rig. Since then we've grown to seven rigs."

All of the rigs work within a 100-mile radius of Hobbs and most of them are west of town. This is because there are so many contractors out of Midland.

"It is tougher drilling west of here. We run into everything from Carlsbad Caverns to high-pressure gas. But our rigs are equipped for this type of drilling. Most of our wells are 9,000 feet to 14,000 feet deep.

"This part of the country is ideal for us to do what we know best—drill wells."

Bob says that up in the Rockies or back east you have to worry about the environment, getting timber cut down and what time of year you can use the roads. In many cases, you have to play political games with county commissioners.

"It is the same way drilling offshore. But in this area, our on-bottom time is probably about 75 percent. That is not just Doranco, but all the contractors out here. Of course, I think we will be right up there at the top, partly because all we really have to worry about out here is making hole."

Working with better people and better equipment than ever before, Bob feels that having the right people and the right equipment minimizes the chances of getting into trouble. But if problems do come up, Bob lets his drilling superintendent handle them on the rig-manager level. "I only enter it secondarily. I used to get involved a lot, but not anymore."

c. (Notice: In this exercise, Darin Schmidt's name was misspelled. Students should have checked its spelling in the city directory.)

SPRINGFIELD—The death of his close friend, Jack Springer, more than two years ago may have led Donald Oaks to take his own life, say close friends and family. But nobody knows for sure.

The 17-year-old Springfield youth died at 6 a.m. May 21, about 15 hours after he had graduated from Springfield Central High School. He celebrated the event at a party with friends, and later that evening was on his way to Jack Springer's grave.

"Donny said before the night was over he wanted to go see Jack," said Tanya Oaks, Donny's sister.

But on his way to the grave Oaks lost control of his car and went into a ditch, according to his friend Greg Manning, a passenger in the car. Manning said Oaks then pulled out his knife and was going to slit his wrists. Manning calmed him down and Oaks put the knife away. Oaks was driven home by the police. He walked straight into his room, loaded his .410 shotgun and shot himself in the head with it. Sheriff Sue Fuller arrived and declared it suicide.

Those who knew Oaks say the suicide might be linked to remorse over the death of Springer, who was killed in a truck accident. Oaks was with him at the time.

He never came to grips with his friend's death, both Ms. Oaks and her mother said.

"I guess he just couldn't take it no more," his mother said.

According to Ms. Oaks, Oaks and Springer were inseparable. They fished, hunted, rode bikes and did everything together. And when Springer died, Oaks really never understood why.

"Donny would let it build up in him," his sister said, "and then he would take it out on things by hitting them. At parties, he'd get upset with it and start hitting things . . . walls, posts, people, whatever."

Oaks's girlfriend, Linda Turner, said that he had been upset the whole week before he died. Oaks told her that he was going to kill himself that Saturday. "I'm going to get the job done, one way or another, and nobody's going to stop me," he told his sister.

She didn't take him seriously. "I just didn't give it much thought."

Other friends of his saw no signs. "If he was having depressed feelings," Darin Schmidt said, "he sure wasn't showing them. Donny was usually cheerful. He seemed to be in a good mood on graduation night."

Another friend, Brad Baumer, said Oaks talked about Jack Springer a lot.

For Oaks, memories weren't enough, so he decided to join his friend since his friend couldn't join him, his family sadly concluded.

"After the accident, he just didn't care," his sister said. "He wanted Jack there no matter what."

Oaks was buried May 23 in the Walnut Ridge Cemetery.

d. Brennan Scanlon hit four 3-pointers in the third quarter, as Springfield's boys' basketball team overcame a 32-25 halftime deficit en route to a 54-43 victory Saturday night in the MFA Oil/Break Time Shootout.

Scanlon, a sophomore guard, finished with a game-high 23 points—14 in the second half. Bruins senior forward Travis Rudloff scored 12 points and had eight rebounds.

"We did a nice job of taking away what they did the first half," said Jim Scanlon, Springfield coach and Brennan's father. "We went with a quicker team and increased our pressure a little bit, and it paid off for us."

Hickman (9-9) hit 5-of-17 shots (29.4 percent) for the final half.

Coach Scanlon had special praise for his seniors, Skyler Graves, Travis Rudloff and Demetrius Thompson.

Senior center Jason Meyer and junior guard Shaun Coleman led Hickman with seven points each.

"We forgot to guard Brennan Scanlon," Hickman coach David Johnson said. "We just totally broke down in every phase of the game in the second half. We didn't execute our half-court offense and didn't play any defense."

With 4:15 left and Springfield leading 45-39, Meyer drove the baseline from the left for a layup. But he was called for charging, and the basket did not count. Johnson said that missed opportunity snapped the Kewpies' momentum.

"I thought he had a good shot. I thought he was in good position, but the referee saw it differently."

The lead never was larger than six in the first quarter, and both teams led.

The second quarter was a quarter of runs. Hickman had an 8-0 run to lead 23-19. Then Springfield regained the lead 25-23 with a 6-0 run. But the Bruins (9-5) didn't score again in the half.

"They hurt us on the offensive boards the first half," coach Scanlon said. "That was probably the difference in the first half."

e. SPRINGFIELD—The purple color of Flat Branch Creek near Fourth and Locust streets probably will pose no environmental hazard.

Firefighters were alerted to the water's color by an unidentified neighbor about 9:30 a.m. Wednesday. Fire Chief Bernard Perry of the Springfield Fire Department said the stream was contaminated by neutralized muriatic acid, which is a dilution of hydrochloric acid.

Perry said the contamination had been emitted from MSA Inc. at 201 S. Seventh St. The corporation used the chemicals to clean its air-conditioning unit, and the residue flowed into the creek by way of a storm drain.

Bob Channey, a university professor of chemical engineering, said muriatic acid is extremely dangerous. "Muriatic acid can burn your skin off," Channey said.

Even the fumes are dangerous, according to Channey.

However, Perry said neutralized muriatic acid probably poses no danger to human health. The purple color, the battalion chief said, was the result of a warning chemical that was mixed with the acid; once the dye is in the purple stage, the hazardous qualities of the acid normally are no longer present.

"The liquid changes into purple when it does everything it can do," Perry said.

Another professor of engineering, John Connors, agreed with Perry. "It's still an acid, but once it's in a stream, the water neutralizes it."

The acid got into the stream because the Ed More Co. used it to clean MSA's air conditioner, said Mike Bangle, MSA's communications coordinator. "From what I understand, it's not caustic," Bangle said.

Nor is it clear that anyone broke the law, Art Crowner of the state Department of Natural Resources said. He promised a thorough investigation.

Perry said the city's drinking water is not in danger. "We get our water from wells, not from Flat Branch Creek."

4. a. All they are saying is give peace a chance.

Committed to the teachings of Jesus Christ, Pax Christi is a group of people who aim to contribute to world peace through prayer, reflection on Scripture and service. The Catholic organization was founded at the end of World War II by a French bishop named Theas.

The local chapter of Pax Christi began over two years ago.

Members are involved in various service ministries, such as St. Francis House, a hospitality center, and Loaves and Fishes, a soup kitchen.

"There's a real neat network of people in Springfield that help people through the different organizations in the community," says Amy Schmidt, local Pax Christi contact. "It's the type of group that can attend to the needs of local people."

The group's members also address broader issues.

"We balance what we do in peace work with work in social justice," says five-year member Lana Jacobs, who also volunteers at Loaves and Fishes.

Pam McClure, who has been involved with the group for a year and a half, agrees.

"The whole thing is an idea of service, self-knowledge . . . putting meaning where it is needed," she says. "I think it is meaningful to take prayer to missile silos, and take prayer and work to St. Francis and the soup kitchen."

Although Pax Christi works for social justice, the group does not directly engage in politics.

"Many groups are politically affiliated, but that's not where I come from," Schmidt says.

"We don't look at what is politically effective, but what's felt in the heart as prayerful," Jacobs explains. "We do what we feel called to do by our spirituality."

Jacobs, who has been involved in the peace movement for 20 years, says politically oriented groups burn out faster than those based on religious tradition.

"People get their strength from their spirituality, be it Buddhist, Christian or whatever," she confides.

Although Pax Christi is a Catholic organization, Schmidt says its catholicity is essentially in terms of "universal." It is a broad coalition of persons concerned with justice who support nonviolence as an alternative to war and violent resistance.

McClure, an Episcopalian, says there are no real differences in perspective because she is not Catholic.

"We're very committed to being rooted in Christ," McClure says. "The call of the Gospel is to preach love, justice and freedom—to help bring the Kingdom of God."

Schmidt says this call has ramifications for the community, the state, the country and the world. The Bible indicates that all things will be in harmony and all relationships will be in order when the kingdom arrives.

"When we become equals, when we're treated equally no matter who we are, that's when the kingdom will be here."

Along with a just world order, Pax Christi's priorities are disarmament, primacy of conscience, education for peace and alternatives to violence.

Disarmament and primacy of conscience, which is mainly concerned with conscientious objection, are the two primary concerns of the local chapter of Pax Christi.

"If you don't address those, you won't have a world left to address them in," says Jacobs.

Although members wish to avert nuclear war, they are concerned mainly with the poor being currently hurt by the arms race.

"Our focus on disarmament is not because of fear of nuclear war, but on the harm it's doing to people now," Schmidt says. "When you see people suffering and you realize nuclear arms are expendable, you know things need to change."

According to Pax Christi literature, 50 million malnourished children in developing countries could be adequately fed for the estimated cost of the MX missile. In addition, 65,000 health-care centers and 340,000 primary schools could be built.

Although many of the organization's concerns have political dimensions, Pax Christi members concentrate on witnessing and prayer, rather than appealing directly to government officials.

The group's members realize that much work remains to be done regarding their objectives.

"There's still injustice in correctional institutions, the arms race is still going on, there's still capital punishment and the draft," Schmidt says. "But I know people have been touched and changed."

b. The early morning sunlight casts his shadow on the ground, as OATS driver Carl Hockman conscientiously checks under the hood of bus 175 and inspects its engine.

Glancing at his watch to ensure punctuality, Hockman boards the bus. After adjusting mirrors and latching his seat belt, he turns the ignition key and begins his route through central Logan County.

With a secure grip on the steering wheel, Hockman adeptly avoids potholes as the bus rolls over the gravel of the winding country roads. This particular yellow bus, labeled OATS in blue, is only one of the 160 vans that provide rural transportation service to 88 counties.

OATS, formally called Older Adult's Transportation Service, is primarily a rural system designed to meet the needs of low-income, elderly or handicapped riders. The service is open to the general public as well.

Entering the driveway of his first passenger of the day, Hockman honks his horn and brings the vehicle to a halt. At each stop, he gets out of the van, preparing to aid his rider in any way he can.

With a pleasant "good morning to ya" and a wide smile, Hockman escorts Mabel Caldwell to the bus door.

"Now Carl, you know that you don't need to get out and help me," she scolds appreciatively.

Refusing to deny his rider the usual courtesies, Hockman opens the door and helps her board the bus. The door of the bus is shut, but only after it is apparent that her seat belt is secure and that she is seated comfortably.

"I look after these women like an old hen with her little chickens," Hockman says proudly.

Guaranteeing personalized service to all their riders, OATS drivers assist passengers in boarding and disembarking. Drivers are given initial orientation on the needs of the elderly and the handicapped. In addition to being trained to handle wheelchairs, they learn defensive driving, first aid and cardiopulmonary resuscitation.

"Oh, Carl, Bonnie's not going today," Ms. Caldwell says. "She says she's got the sniffles."

Hockman patiently revises his route and then maneuvers the bus throughout central Logan County to pick up other passengers—Ruth, Maxine, Enid, Vera and Nancy.

Ruth, who is waiting patiently inside, hears the horn blow and hurries out to the bus. As she climbs aboard, her dog yelps loudly, objecting to its master's departure.

"That's OK," says Hockman, assuring the barking dog. "We'll be sure and bring her back safe and sound."

The riders are gradually picked up and greetings are exchanged between friends, as the bus is transformed into a moving social center with women discussing events of the past week.

News about a friend in the hospital generates immediate concern among the riders, and plans are made to buy her a card. The group wave as they pass by the house of a woman who was unable to join them that day.

The brightness of the sun that is peeking out from behind the overshadowing clouds complements the good cheer of the talkative women. Birds chirp loudly and green buds indicate spring's arrival.

"Praise the Lord for this beautiful day," Hockman shouts as he inhales the fresh country air.

"Isn't it wonderful to hear them old frogs a-croakin' again?" Maxine asks.

Heads nod in agreement; it's good to be "out and about" on such a nice day.

"The OATS buses mean so much to so many people," Hockman shouts over the rumbling of voices in the background. "It's the only form of transportation that some of these people have."

OATS helps the elderly or handicapped individual meet his or her transportation needs independently, without having to burden friends, relatives or neighbors. For some elderly, this door-to-door bus service serves as an alternative to a nursing home.

Offering the chance to meet new people, OATS also helps to alleviate the loneliness that often results from living in isolated, rural areas.

"Some passengers own a car but like to ride along just to see their friends," Hockman says. "It's a form of therapy and breaks the monotony of looking at bare walls."

As the bus enters the city limits, the women skim through newspaper ads in order to determine where the best bargains can be found. Hockman attempts to make sense out of the confusion as six women blurt out the various errands to be done.

"Now, do we have any doctor's appointments today?" Hockman asks with clipboard in hand.

Much to everyone's relief, none has been scheduled for that day.

The trip becomes lengthy when several passengers have appointments to meet.

"Oh, Carl, I need to stop at the pharmacist's to get some prescriptions refilled," Enid says.

Regular service includes trips for shopping, medical or essential business purposes, and to visit senior centers and nutrition sites. Today, stops are made at two banks and grocery stores, and at the Biscayne Mall.

"You can go this trip a dozen times, and none would be the same," Hockman says as he drops Nancy off at Nowell's. The others discuss plans for lunch.

"I'll pick you up at 1 p.m.," Hockman assures Nancy.

"Now is that going to give you enough time to do all of your shopping?" Hockman asks.

Hockman helps Nancy off the bus and into the store. Meanwhile, the decision about lunch is proving difficult; six different people opt for their favorite restaurants.

The deliberations continue as each rider presents her preference. The compromise is made. The group will eat cafeteria-style in order to satisfy everyone's palate.

"There's times when you just have to bear with the crowd," Hockman says, attempting to comfort those who didn't get their choice.

After lunch, the riders stop at Biscayne Mall and are given a designated time to meet. All go their separate ways, weaving in and out of the shops, purchasing what they need.

At 3 p.m., Hockman's bus waits at the front of the mall. Five weary shoppers, laden with packages, come filing out and approach the bus.

"What all did you get today, Enid?" Ruth asks, as the two women discuss the sales they came across.

In order to account for all of his passengers, Hockman begins to count heads. One . . . two . . . three . . . four . . . five . . .?

It soon becomes apparent that No. 6 is missing, so Hockman heads out to round up the last member of his crew.

"Carl is so patient with us," Enid says.

The women agree and then try to determine the whereabouts of their missing friend. After 10 minutes of searching, Hockman returns with the late rider.

"It's a good thing we found her," Hockman teases. "I was about to drive home without her."

On the way home, the bus is crowded with groceries and other cumbersome packages. The once-bright sunlight has dimmed, reflecting the flagging energy of the women.

Gradually, the bus empties, and the cheerful voices of the passengers are replaced by the sound of gravel spitting out from under the tires.

c. When it comes to a person's family tree, many of us are content with a sapling.

But there are some who want to know their roots.

Virginia Nichols of 115 Lake St., a descendant of Cedric, King of West Saxony, A.D. 519 to 534, is one of those people.

She became interested in her genealogy in 1975 following the death of her father. While checking his safe-deposit box, she came across an application for the Daughters of the War of 1812 that her maternal grandmother had partly filled out.

Nichols is currently a member of about 20 genealogical organizations. They include Daughters of the American Revolution, National Society of Americans of Royal Descent, Dames of the Court of Honor, Magna Carta Dames, Descendants of Emperor Charlemagne, Order of the First Three Crusades and Daughters of the War of 1812.

A friend who had done some research on Nichols' ancestors helped her get started on what is now an impressive collection of names and dates.

"He supplied me with some information but no proof," she says, "so I had to start backtracking in order to get proof."

Nichols began work on her husband's genealogy at the same time. "My ancestors came to the Ashland area in 1818 and his in 1823. We have not one mutual ancestor as far as I've been able to trace," Nichols says.

In order to get into each genealogical society, one must have proof of an ancestor from the particular time periods, Nichols says. Often one ancestor will get an individual into more than one organization.

Organizations generally require a copy of an individual's birth certificate and marriage license as well as his or her parents' marriage license, in addition to a copy, if possible, of a legal document proving the ancestor's existence. Nichols says most organizations will accept a published listing that includes the ancestors as proof.

"The ultimate organization to be able to join was the Order of the First Three Crusades," she says. "I have five ancestors who were members of the first crusade. You could only file on one, so I filed on Hugh Magnum, who was a duke of Normandy and the son of King Henry II of France."

Nichols has also proved to be a descendant of 14 of the barons who signed the Magna Carta in 1215. She explained that 17 of those who signed have descendants. She's still working on the other three.

"King John Lackland of England was forced by the barons to sign the document, and I have proved I'm a descendant of his, even if he was a scoundrel," Nichols says, laughing.

Opening one of her many historical books, she flips to a page listing the council of 1619. Beside the name Edward Gourgany she has written the word "mine."

"I'm basically just trying to find as many names as possible," she says. She's looking for husbands and wives, where they were born, where and when they died. In other words, she's trying to establish the surname line.

"The way things are going now, many places are destroying records. If you don't get this down somewhere, it's going to be lost to future generations."

Having experienced the process of tracing her family tree, Nichols offers some advice for the beginner.

"Begin with yourself and work backwards. You don't want to start with an important person and work down. So many people want to belong to someone famous like George Washington, and of course, he didn't have any children so you'll be stymied right there.

"You must prove each step. You'll have blank spots, but you don't guess. If you do, put it in pencil, which says, 'This is an idea, but it may not be right.'"

Nichols says that locally she has found the state Historical Society to be helpful in her endeavors. James Goodrich, associate director of the library, says the library is a key depository for individuals to begin researching their family trees.

"We have over 400,000 volumes of history," he explains. "This includes many books on the history of different counties and cities as well as family histories."

The library also has the largest state newspaper collection in the nation. Its collection of state census records from 47 states can obviously be of great use to those who want to learn about their past.

Nichols says that in addition to reference materials, she gets much of her information from published inquiries she submits to different publications.

"I also write letters to people all over the United States," she says. "I even correspond with people in Alaska and Hawaii. I help them and they help me.

"Through these years I have had a lot of hits and misses and so have done some unnecessary work and still do," Nichols says. "The nice part is I feel like I've made so many friends by correspondence."

5. Choosing the best sentences to quote here should arouse good discussion. Quotations to be considered:

"Our schools are producing a nation of economic illiterates!" (This is an attention-getting quotation.)

"Just 39 percent knew what the Gross National Product measures." (The GNP is a regular part of the news. That only a third of our students know what it is is shocking.)

"Students should take a course in economics before they graduate from high school." (This is a startling statement if we consider that many graduate from college without completing a course in economics.)

"Our nation cannot afford to have high school students who lack the basic skills to understand vital economic issues." (This quotation, combined with the next one, drives home the realization that we are not competing and will not be able to compete with other nations such as Japan.)

"All high school students in Japan are required to take economics."

6. Comparing how the professionals cover the news is both interesting and informative. This assignment also forces students to read newspapers. The assignment need not be for stories about the president, but they are usually frequent and easy to find. It is striking how often professionals will choose the same quotes.

7. **CHALLENGE EXERCISE.**
   a. You would do best to send the whole class to the same meeting. That way you will be able to compare students' work in class. The exercise also trains students in how to get direct quotes. Comparing their accuracy is also most useful. If your local paper covers the meeting, you have something else to compare students' work with.

b.-c. Again, this exercise will help students judge worthwhile quotes and train them to record them accurately.

CHAPTER 5: GATHERING INFORMATION

Overview

This chapter is intended to serve as an introduction to the basic sources of information available to reporters, but it emphasizes an important new source of information—online computer databases.

No modern reporter can expect to be successful without learning to use electronic sources of information. That begins with use of the electronic library or morgue found at almost any newspaper and at many broadcast stations. Today, however, most newspapers and broadcast stations also have access to various commercial databases that are invaluable in providing background for a story. It is essential for the young reporter to learn to use them.

The exercises that accompany this chapter are designed to help acquaint your students with the vast array of information available online. If you do not have access to the commercial databases or cannot allow student access to them because of the cost, use the Internet for the same purpose. Voluminous databases are available free on the Internet from almost any college or university.

Solutions to Textbook Questions and Exercises

1. Students should be required to consider all possible sources for a story. An objective evaluation of another reporter's story is a good way to start this thought process.
2. An obvious source of information for anyone familiar with databases would be Dow Jones News Retrieval, which contains vast amounts of material on large, publicly traded companies such as Apple Computer. Of course, many traditional sources of information also are available.
3. It is amazing how much information is readily available on people such as U.S. senators. A good place to start is the state manuals issued by most states. Extensive biographical sketches of the state's U.S. senators usually are included. The local newspaper library is another obvious source of material. Senators who have been in office for some time will have extensive biographical data included in manuals, such as *Who's Who in America*, and various government reference works. In short, this is an easy assignment. Thoroughness is the key to doing it well.
4. Navigating the Internet is merely a matter of finding a good place to start. For information provided by U.S. government agencies, go to an excellent site maintained by EINet Corp. (http://galaxy.einet.net). You can use that as the starting point for agency information that will answer the first three questions.
   a. Rhode Island's population in 2000 was 1,048,319 (U.S. Census Bureau World Wide Web site).
   b. Rwanda's land area is 10,169 square miles *(CIA World Fact Book)*.
   c. Awards by the U.S. Department of Education can be found at its Web site (www.ed.gov).

d. Norwegian institutions with a presence on the Internet include the universities of Bergen, Oslo, Tromsoe and Trondheim. Other institutions also have a presence. Any Internet search engine will take you to a list of Norwegian sites.

e. The complete works of William Shakespeare appear at several sites on the Internet. To begin searching, go to the Shakespeare Web site (http://www.shakespeare.com). For those without that site information, a WebCrawler search of the Internet should help locate the site.

f. As of this writing, there is no centralized location for campaign contribution information. However, some watchdog agencies (such as Common Cause) are beginning to post that information (see the Common Cause Web site—www.commoncause.com). Other campaign contribution information may be posted by various foundations with specific areas of interest.

Solutions to Workbook Questions and Exercises

1. The simple way to find the answer to this question is to check your local phone book. The number of the nearest INS office should be included. A phone call should yield the mailing and e-mail addresses. The same information can be found in your college or university library in a number of places. Try the phone book for the nearest large city or enlist the help of the librarian, who can point you to several possible sources. Some state manuals (often called *Blue Books*) also include information about federal agencies.

2. The U.S. Army Corps of Engineers controls major inland rivers in the United States and would be a major source of information about flood control. The Federal Emergency Management Agency might provide information about damage during the most recent flood on the river. The U.S. Department of Agriculture might provide information about crop losses. State emergency management and state agriculture departments would be other good sources. There may be many others.

3. This is a good exercise to teach students how to use a city directory. Unlike phone books, city directories, published for most large and medium-sized cities, contain information about a person's occupation in addition to his or her phone number and address. Students also could be sent to the local newspaper library to find answers to this question.

4. Complete biographical data for these individuals can be found on Lexis/Nexis or in various *Who's Who* publications. The following are brief identifications for them:

   a. Henry Aaron, vice president of the Atlanta Braves and baseball's all-time home run champion.

   b. Sandra Day O'Connor, a U.S. Supreme Court justice and the first woman named to that court.

   c. Tom Harkin, Democratic senator from Iowa.

   d. Pete Sampras, at one time a highly ranked tennis player from the United States.

   e. Richard Petty, a NASCAR stock-car driver.

   f. Venus Williams, a professional tennis player.

   g. Barbara Boxer, Democratic senator from California.

h. Colin Powell, U.S. Secretary of State in 2004 and former chairman of the Joint Chiefs of Staff.

i. Kim Dae-Jung, president of South Korea.

j. Jay Leno, host of NBC's *Tonight* show.

k. Alani Apio, a Hawaiian playwright, sculptor and actor from the island of Oahu.

l. Bill Bradley, former Democratic senator from New Jersey and former presidential candidate.

m. John Chaney, coach of the Temple University basketball team.

n. Tiger Woods, professional golfer.

o. David Justice, professional baseball player.

5. a. The final popular vote in the 2000 presidential election was Al Gore, 50,999,897; George W. Bush, 50,456,002; and Ralph Nader, 2,882,995.

   b. The electoral vote was Bush, 271; Gore, 266.

6. U.S. senators (effective 2004):

   a. Florida: Bob Graham (D) and Bill Nelson (D)

   b. Kansas: Sam Brownback (R) and Pat Roberts (R)

   c. Tennessee: Lamar Alexander (R) and Bill Frist (R)

   d. New Mexico: Pete V. Domenici (R) and Jeff Bingaman (D)

   e. Washington: Patty Murray (D) and Maria Cantwell (D)

   f. California: Barbara Boxer (D) and Dianne Feinstein (D)

   g. Illinois: Richard Durbin (D) and Peter Fitzgerald (R)

   h. New York: Charles Schumer (D) and Hillary Rodham Clinton (D)

   i. Maine: Susan Collins (R) and Olympia J. Snowe (R)

   j. North Carolina: Elizabeth Dole (R) and John Edwards (D)

7. Largest cities:

   a. New Hampshire: Manchester

   b. Connecticut: Bridgeport

   c. Mississippi: Jackson

   d. Utah: Salt Lake City

   e. Colorado: Denver

   f. Alabama: Birmingham

   g. Iowa: Des Moines

   h. Ohio: Columbus

   i. Kentucky: Louisville

   j. North Dakota: Fargo

8. The last five prime ministers of Canada:

   a. Paul Martin, 2003-present

   b. Jean Chrétien, 1993-2003

   c. Kim Campbell, 1993

   d. Brian Mulroney, 1984-1993

   e. John Turner, 1984

9. Primary cash crops:

   a. India: rice

   b. Germany: grain, potatoes

   c. Kenya: coffee

   d. Romania: corn, wheat

   e. Canada: wheat

   f. Colombia: coffee

   g. Argentina: cotton, grains

h. Egypt: cotton
i. Mongolia: grain
j. New Zealand: grain
10. There should be ample sources of information about when your city was incorporated. A check with city hall or the local library should produce the answer quickly; so might a brochure from the chamber of commerce. U.S. Census figures or city offices can provide information about the most recent census data. That information is available in computer databases for recent censuses. Data for older ones will have to be obtained from libraries or city offices.
11. a. Telephone book and city directory.
   b. The county recorder of deeds.
   c. The tax assessor.
   d. Biographical data from the mayor's office, newspaper clippings or friends and neighbors.
   e. The tax assessor.
12. This information is filed with the federal government on various Form 990 and 10K reports. It is available in many online services, including Dow Jones News Retrieval.
13. Stock prices are found on almost all the commercial database services. If your students lack access to those, a stockbroker or *The Wall Street Journal* can provide the same information.
14. This exercise is a good one for teaching students that there are many ways to write a story. Critical examination of the approaches taken by two reporters is an excellent way to learn how to evaluate the quality of newswriting.
15. The best choice might be Dow Jones News Retrieval because of the nature of the story. However, expect good results from Lexis/Nexis too. Its exhaustive lists of magazines and newspapers mean that you'll almost certainly find an answer.
16. There are several trade magazines published for the grocery industry. These would be good sources of information. Almost any of the major online database services also would provide good information about the grocery business.
17. The fast-food industry is a difficult one to tackle. People who are willing to talk about profits in that sector are rare. However, it should be possible to check with your city finance office to see how much each store in your area paid in taxes. Those figures will relate directly to sales. The commercial database services also will provide plenty of background information.
18. A. Obvious sources of information:
   a. Springfield University Extension Service
   b. David Baker, Extension Service safety specialist
   c. Jan Hedeman, president, Dade County Extension Council
   d. Rusty Lee, state extension associate
   Other sources that might have been used include the federal Occupational Safety and Health Administration, the Department of Agriculture and nearby college or university safety experts.
   B. Obvious sources of information:
   a. Springfield Red Cross

b. George Glenn, city fire marshal
c. Gena Pliske, Red Cross official
Other sources that might have been used include owners of near-by homes and businesses, the fire and police chiefs, and ambulance officials.
C. Obvious sources of information:
a. Diane Lusbey, city manager
b. Nicole Ziden, Lincoln County commissioner
c. Andrew Kramer, Lincoln County commissioner
d. Jeanne Matten, local businessperson
e. Jose Rodriguez, assistant city manager
Other possible sources:
a. Downtown business association
b. Chamber of commerce
c. Les Dally architectural firm
19. Information about director and producer Steven Spielberg is easily obtained from *Who's Who* or from the Lexis/Nexis database of famous people. Any commercial database also would contain stories about him, including profiles.
20. **CHALLENGE EXERCISE.** Shaquille O'Neal's business dealings have been the topic of numerous stories. Any commercial database should provide plenty of information on the subject. This exercise could be done with almost any famous individual.

CHAPTER 6: REPORTING WITH NUMBERS

Overview

The dearth of math skills among journalists is so well-known that many people in the profession joke that they chose the field in order to avoid math. This attitude, of course, reflects not only an ignorance about performing basic calculations but also an ignorance of the ways of the world.

Changes in budget figures reflect changing priorities in government, in agencies and even in entire cultures. Per capita spending (or saving) often tells a more accurate story of funding levels than total budgets do. Percentages and percentage changes reflect proportions. Averages and medians can sometimes reflect important comparisons and contrasts behind issues in the news.

This chapter presents both the issues and the formulas involved in many basic news stories. Even the most math-phobic students should be able to follow along using the basic skills of adding, subtracting, multiplying and dividing. Slogging through the exercises with the help of the formulas provided will help students gain confidence in evaluating numbers on the job.

Solutions to Textbook Questions and Exercises

1. The debt of the average college student is computed by dividing the total debt by the number of full-time equivalent (FTE) students. The average debt of the indebted student is calculated by dividing the total debt by the number of FTE students with loans.

The exercise gives the class a chance to see that several important distinctions arise when the numbers are calculated one way versus another. Computing the debt load of indebted students is a more accurate portrayal of students with loans, and it also will give people a sense of how much of the student body is walking away with that burden.

Financial aid officials will likely remind students that the total of the Stafford Loans is not a picture of all student debt. Other loan programs are available, families often lend students money, and increasing numbers of college students are graduating with heavy credit card debt as well.

2. Tell your students to consult www.bls.gov/cpi. From there, students click on "Get Detailed CPI Statistics," then "All Urban Consumers (Current Series)," then "U.S. Education and Communication, 1982-84" to get CPI figures. To adjust for inflation, get the CPI for the current year (the figures are given monthly; use the latest available) and the CPI for the appropriate periods.

The result is what the tuition from 1994 on would be today after it is adjusted for inflation. This is the only fair comparison to today's tuition. The point is that there's no way to make a fair comparison without adjusting for inflation.

You may want to urge students to use common sense when thinking about the Consumer Price Index and the calculations involved. The CPI is nothing more than a mathematical tool that helps relate the changes in the cost of living from year to year. The formula is so simple that the results of the calculation will be logical (i.e., the tuition in 1994 will be higher after it is adjusted for inflation). If it is not higher, students need to go back to the formula to make sure they did the proper calculation.

Writing a story about the trends in college costs will give students a clearer idea about the changes, and perhaps show them that many services are available now that were not available 20 or 30 years ago. It should also be easy for students to track alumni from the classes of 1950 and 1960 through the alumni association, and many of them will probably have crystal-clear memories of how much they paid for tuition.

If you don't want them to work the calculation themselves, refer students to the Web site: www.newsengin.com.

3. Many big metropolitan papers do a good job of writing clearly about numbers, but many more papers do not. Students should use parallel construction in their writing and try to simplify terms as much as possible. For example, they should not use *40 percent* one time and *two out of five* in another case. The students should put incomprehensible numbers into some kind of context (i.e., "The governor's budget totals $347 million, *about $300 for every resident of the state*.").

Young journalists who go to the effort of calculating a lot of figures sometimes feel the need to follow the "shovel" method of writing. "Well, I went to all the trouble," they think, "I'm going to shovel all those figures in there." Remind students that running the numbers is a good way for them to get a handle on things. Gaining that insight will help them be better storytellers but not if they're bent on jamming every statistic into the story. They need to pick out the highlights and the best ways to illustrate the story.

4. One of the most important things for students to notice in comparative tables of any kind is that people need to compare apples to apples. Students

need to make sure they convert the raw numbers to *per student* so that they can properly compare them from campus to campus. If your campus has 20,000 students and there were 320 thefts, the per capita rate would be .016 thefts per student (not very helpful) or 16 thefts for every thousand students. (Obtain that more illustrative change by multiplying by 1,000.) That's also one of every 62 students.

If another campus had 8,000 students and 120 thefts, the per capita rate would be 120 ÷ 8,000, or .015 thefts per student. The smaller campus has 15 thefts for every 1,000 students, about the same proportion as the bigger campus.

Also, have students discuss what different numbers might mean on different campuses, and what they might not mean. What about a campus that has a high number of alcohol- or drug-related offenses? Does that mean alcohol and drug use is high? Might it mean that enforcement is stricter? Perhaps recordkeeping methods are different. The point is that numbers can tell a lot, but comparisons are helpful only when they take a variety of factors into account. Understanding those factors is the only way to make stories accurate, balanced and fair.

5. The questions will depend on the specific budget the reporter is analyzing. In general, you ask for causes any time a budget item goes up or down at a faster rate than the overall budget. For instance, if the budget proposal is for an overall increase of 3 percent, question each increase that is significantly larger than 3 percent. Within each department, look for notable increases. It might lead you to equipment purchases, for instance, or to increases in employees. Also question any significant decreases.

In addition, look at the figures by department over at least five years to see if there are any trends. You may find a change in priorities, stated or unstated.

Ask questions of your council and managers about their priorities. Compare the responses to the budget, which is a numerical reflection of the priorities.

Also be sure to adjust for inflation. An increase of 3 percent will probably be a budget that is flat. It would reflect increasing costs of goods and services. Look at the impact of inflation over a five-year period too.

Solutions to Workbook Questions and Exercises

1. The important thing for students to understand about this budget is that tuition and fees comprise only a small portion of the money it takes to run this college. Six million dollars in tuition may seem like a lot, but it is a tiny fraction of the total, most of which is borne by taxpayers.

a. To figure percentages of the total budget, divide portion by the whole:

$80 million ÷ $120 million = .667, or 67 percent
$6 million ÷ $120 million = .05, or 5 percent
$34 million ÷ $120 million = .28, or 28 percent

b. Two-thirds, or 67 percent, of the college's $120 million budget comes from state taxpayers. Fees, grants and gifts make up the next most important source of funding, accounting for 28 percent of the budget. Tuition accounts for only a small part of the total budget—just 5 percent.

c. The college's budget comes mostly from state taxpayers, who pay two-thirds of the costs. Fees, grants and gifts pay a little more than one-quarter of the costs. Student tuition pays for just $1 of every $20 spent for the college.

2. The important thing for reporters to notice about the mayor's attack on the Republican congressional candidate is that it makes no attempt to portray what proportion of the total votes cast during a legislative year the candidate missed, nor does it compare the candidate's performance with those of others.

   a. To write a balanced story, a journalist would need to know what percentage of votes cast during the last legislative year the candidate missed and how the candidate's attendance record compares with those of others in Congress. Possible sources include the incumbent member of Congress, her press secretary, a local political science professor and past members of Congress.

   b. To find the number of roll-call votes on the Internet, go to:

   http://lcweb.loc.gov/global/legislative/congress.html

3. The purpose of this exercise in interpreting budgets is to show how simple calculations can shed light on numbers that can be difficult to compare at first blush. For example, Springfield has by far the largest budget and the biggest budget increase in raw dollars of any of the four school districts surveyed. But calculating per capita spending and percentage increases in students and budgets shows that Springfield is adding just enough money in the new budget to maintain its current level of spending per student.

   At the same time, Middletown is maintaining the same budget as in the previous year, but the student body is becoming much larger. Middletown's per capita spending plummets, but it still has the highest per capita spending of any of the districts.

   In these cases, the numbers help the reporter see how finances are changing so that he or she can do a better job of telling what's going on.

   a. Per capita spending = total budget ÷ number of students

	1999	2000
Springfield	$23,250,000 ÷ 4,650 $5,000/student	$23,620,000 ÷ 4,724 $5,000/student
Newburg	$12,787,500 ÷ 2,325 $5,500/student	$12,991,000 ÷ 2,362 $5,500/student
Hampton	$4,450,425 ÷ 1,211 $3,675/student	$3,496,000 ÷ 1,101 $3,175/student
Middletown	$7,530,000 ÷ 1,004 $7,500/student	$7,530,000 ÷ 1,213 $6,208/student

   b. Percentage change in per capita spending.

   Step 1: [new spending – old spending] ÷ old spending level
   Step 2: Move decimal point two places to the right.

Springfield	No change
Newburg	No change

Hampton | $3,175 - $3,675 = -$500
-$500 ÷ $3,675 = -.136
= 13.6% drop in spending per student

Middletown | $6,208 - $7,500 = -$1,292
-$1,292 ÷ $7,500 = -.172
= 17.2% decline in spending per student

4. a. Percentage change in students.

Step 1: [new number of students – old number of students] ÷ [old number]

Step 2: Move decimal point two spaces to the right.

Springfield | 4,724 – 4,650 = 74
74 ÷ 4,650 = .0159
= 1.6% increase in number of students

Newburg | 2,362 – 2,325 = 37
37 ÷ 2,325 = .0159
= 1.6% increase in number of students

Hampton | 1,101 – 1,211 = –110
–110 ÷ 1,211 = –.0908
= 9.1% drop in number of students

Middletown | 1,213 – 1,004 = 209
209 ÷ 1,004 = .208
= 20.8% increase in number of students

b. Percentage change in budgets.

Step 1: [new budget – old budget] ÷ old budget

Step 2: Move decimal point two spaces to the right.

Springfield | $23,620,000 – $23,250,000 = $370,000
$370,000 ÷ $23,250,000 = .0159
= 1.6% increase in the budget

Newburg | $12,991,000 – $12,787,500 = $203,500
$203,500 ÷ $12,787,500 = .0159
= 1.6% increase in the budget

Hampton | $3,496,000 – $4,450,425 = –$954,425
–$954,425 ÷ $4,450,425 = –.214
= 21.4% cut in the budget

Middletown | No change

5. Area school districts face a variety of circumstances. Springfield and Newburg are seeing relatively small increases in their student bodies and are increasing their budgets just enough to maintain the same level of spending as last year.

Middletown, the area's best-financed school district, is experiencing an influx of students, with more than 200 students enrolling over last year's figure of about 1,000. The budget will remain the same as last year, and as a result the district's per capita spending will plummet from $7,500 per student to $6,208 per student. Even with this 17 percent drop, Middletown still spends far more money per child than any other area school district.

In Hampton, the student body is shrinking, but the budget is shrinking even more. The number of students will fall by 110, from about 1,200 to about 1,100, and the budget will fall nearly $1 million, to about $3.5 million, a 21 percent drop from last year.

To help round out the story and explain the trends in area school budgets, reporters would certainly want to know what is causing fluctuations in enrollments. It might be the addition of new housing developments in Middletown, the opening of a factory or office center that is attracting a lot of families with children all of a sudden, or maybe even a vote by Middletown to annex part of Hampton. Reporters would obviously like to know how changes in per capita spending are going to be made up. Will class sizes increase? Will artistic offerings, such as art and music classes, still be available? If budget shortages will be made up in part by the retirement of senior teachers, how will that affect the school?

Probable sources are school principals, school board members, PTA officials, teachers and parents. Students involved in extracurricular activities that are threatened with cuts might also be a fruitful source.

6. Seven resident advisers are affected by heavier workloads. That's one of every six RAs on campus. These RAs' dormitory wings, which used to house 18 students, now house 36 each. The RAs are complaining of a 200 percent increase in their workload. Reporters should check their math.

a. Step 1: [new number – old number] ÷ old number
   Step 2: Move decimal point two places to the right.

   $(36 - 18) ÷ 18 = 1.00$, or 100 percent increase

   The RAs' math is faulty. (If they had experienced a 200 percent increase in their workload, each of the RAs affected would have 54 students. Reporters may wish to check if any is a math major.)

   The total number of dormitory residents affected is 252, or 18.6 percent of the 1,357 students living on campus ($252 ÷ 1,357$). That's about one of every five students living on campus.

   Another interesting fact appears if reporters check how many residents the average RA is responsible for.

   1,357 students ÷ 42 RAs = 32 students per RA

   Thus, the RAs who are complaining do have a slightly higher workload than the average RA.

   So it is true that these RAs have seen their workloads double, but the university is still paying them just the same as it does other RAs with similar workloads.

   Part of the truth of the matter lies in financial figures that are not presented. How much of the budget savings is the university passing on to residents? Seven dormitory wings have added 18 residents each, resulting in a total of 252 students. How much do these residents pay for their rooms? How much did the 126 residents pay last year? The university's revenue will have gone up quite a lot, and its expenses will rise somewhat.

b. A tentative lead for the story:

   A group of resident advisers at Springfield University say that the university is unfairly doubling their workload without any change in their pay.

7. a. To calculate the average prison term, convert all the prison sentences to months. Add all the prison terms together and divide by the number of examples.

Kimball	12 months
Pelletier	12 months
Mitchell	14 months
Newberry	12 months
Smith	12 months
Rothstein	8 months
Hamlet	84 months

$12 + 12 + 14 + 12 + 12 + 8 + 84 = 154$

$154 \div 7 = 22$ months = average prison term

b. To calculate the median prison term, plot the figures on a straight line from lowest to highest and identify the figure where half fall above, and half fall below.

8   12   12   <u>12</u>   12   14   84

The median prison term is 12 months.

c. The median prison term is far more accurate than the average, or mean, prison term. The average works out to a little under two years, even though six of the seven examples given were sentenced to a lot less than that.

In this case, it is easily apparent that Michael Hamlet's seven-year prison sentence skews the results. It would probably help illustrate the factors involved in sentencing to look at the criminal records of all the defendants. The district attorney or the judge involved in Hamlet's case might also be able to explain what makes the difference in sentencing.

8. a. After one year, a student borrowing $1,000 will owe:

$1,000 × .03 = $30 in interest plus the principal
$1,030 is the amount owed after one year.

To figure the amount owed after five years:

Principal × (1 + interest rate) {number of years}
$1,000 × (1.03){5} = $1,000 × 1.159
$1,159 is the amount owed after five years.

b. If the student accepts a $1,000 loan for each of her five years in college, she owes a different amount of interest for each $1,000 loan.

For year 1: $1,000 × (1.03){5} = $1,159
For year 2: $1,000 × (1.03){4} = $1,126
For year 3: $1,000 × (1.03){3} = $1,093
For year 4: $1,000 × (1.03){2} = $1,061
For year 5: $1,000 × (1.03) = $1,030
$5,469 = total amount owed

(Notice that this calculation is based on simple interest, a method that will give far different results than standard amortization formulas. Also, government-backed student loans do not charge interest for the years that the student is in school, so interest is not charged until after graduation. Nevertheless, this example illustrates how interest owed adds up over time.)

9. a. To calculate the percentage increase in a cup of coffee at Joe's from $1.00 to $1.25, do the following calculation:

Percent change = [new price – old price] ÷ old price
$1.25 – $1.00 = $.25
.25 ÷ 1.00 = .25, or a 25 percent increase

b. Tell your students to consult the CPI tables available on the World Wide Web through the Bureau of Labor Statistics (www.bls.gov/cpihome. htm). They should choose "data" and "all urban." The most commonly used figures are those making 1967 the "zero" year—the numbers are all adjusted compared to 1967 dollars. (This fact will help in the choice of tables, but it will be immaterial to their calculations.)

To adjust the 1978 cost of a cup of coffee for inflation, do the following calculation. This example uses the average CPI for 2000. You may wish to use the CPI of the current month.

CPI 2000 ÷ CPI 1978 = 172.2 ÷ 65.2 = 2.641. This is the multiplier.
25 cents × 2.641 = 66 cents

A cup of coffee at Joe's would cost 66 cents if Joe had kept pace with inflation. So even after raising his price, Joe is actually charging less for a cup of coffee than when he opened his business 22 years ago.

It may help to point out to students that the math actually makes sense. The multiplier 2.641 means that the cost of things has more than doubled in the past 22 years, which should seem about right.

10. a. Using 2003 data for all U.S. cities (2004 data not available at the time this book was produced), the teachers would be earning $31,090 if their salaries had kept pace with the Consumer Price Index. You can get more specific figures by selecting the area in which you are located when you calculate the figures.

b. Mayor Williams' pride in rising teacher salaries is unfounded. Though salaries have increased $8,000 over the past 12 years, analysis shows that starting salaries actually have declined after adjusting for inflation. If starting salaries were just keeping pace with inflation, new teachers would be earning $29,100 a year. That's $1,100 more than current levels.

c. Mr. Abraham's charge that Mayor Williams is coddling teachers is unfounded. Analysis shows that teacher salaries have declined after adjusting for inflation. Teachers have not seen a pay increase in real terms.

11. a. The total cost of the shirt will increase from $26.50 to $26.75, a 25-cent increase. The tax increases from $1.50 to $1.75.

b. The total cost of the computer will increase from $1,632 to $1,647.80, a $15.80 increase. The tax increases from $92.40 to $107.80.

c. The total cost of a $15,000 car will increase from $15,900 to $16,050, a $150 increase. The tax increases from $900 to $1,050.

d. The impact of a 1 percent increase in the sales tax for the county will vary according to the cost of the product and the inclination to follow price changes. Consumers probably would not cross the county line for the express purpose of saving a quarter on a $25 shirt, but they might shop around to avoid an extra $150 tax on a new car.

To answer this question fully, reporters would need to contact an economist, the state taxation office or other offices that might be able to verify how the tax change would affect spending.

12. a. Assuming a state sales tax of 6 percent, a fast-food patron who spends $5 a week would save 30 cents per week, or $15.60 in a year.

   b. A patron of a more expensive eatery who spends $20 a week eating out would save $1.20 each week, or $62.40 in a year.

13. To determine a property tax:

   Step 1: Find the assessed value, and move the decimal point three spaces to the left.

   Step 2: Take the result from Step 1 and multiply by the millage rate.

   Calculate current property taxes.

   $136,000 × 23.80 = $3,236,800 in property taxes each year

   Calculate property taxes under the mill's proposal.

   $80,000 × 23.80 = $1,904,000 in property taxes each year

   To calculate the lost revenues, subtract the proposed tax payment from the current tax payment.

   $3,236,800 − $1,904,000 = $1,332,800

   The paper mill would see its tax bill lowered by $1,332,800 each year. That's a 41 percent cut.

14. a. Smaller numbers often yield greater percentages. That is true here. The greatest percentage increase is in the smallest category (of those given for all three years)—community services. The percentage is 55 percent.

   b. The Police Department (33 percent) has outgained the Fire Department (30 percent).

   c. Yes, from 61 percent to 62 percent.

15. a. The statement shows an increase in sales tax revenue but a decrease in property tax revenue. The most likely cause is a cut in the property tax rate. Perhaps the sales tax rate was raised too. The best source for this information is the city finance office. The files of your local paper will tell you too.

   b. The General Fund balance comes from transfers from other funds, mainly the Special Revenue Fund, added to the leftover from the $4.2 million balance in the General Fund at the beginning of the year.

16. You'll want to make sure your news conference answers are consistent with the documents, but there's room for creativity. Students' written questions should focus on what the city is buying with its budget increases and on what evidence exists of improved public safety. Students should follow up on the unexplained "series of management changes" and explore the ramifications of the shift from reliance on property taxes to reliance on sales taxes. The stories should draw on the interview, the written statement and the documents. Look for mathematical errors as well as for answers to the questions readers are likely to ask.

17. **CHALLENGE EXERCISE.** This exercise again illustrates that adjusting for inflation is crucial to conveying an accurate story.

   a. To calculate property taxes:

   Step 1: Find the assessed value and move the value of the property three spaces to the left.

Step 2: Take the results of Step 1 and multiply by the millage rate.

65 × 18.75 = $1,219 = taxes paid in 1990 on the median home in Springfield

100 × 18.75 = $1,875 = taxes paid in 2000 on the median home

b. To adjust for inflation, see instructions in previous exercises. Again, this exercise uses the latest monthly figure for 2000. You will want to use the average CPI for the year once it becomes available. Your results will be just about the same.

CPI 2000 ÷ CPI 1990 = 172.2 ÷ 130.7 = 1.318

1.318 × $65,000 = $85,670 would be the price of the median home in Springfield if housing had just kept pace with inflation.

1.318 × $1,219 = $1,606 would be the property tax bill for the median home in Springfield if the assessed value of homes had just kept pace with inflation.

To make an accurate comparison between current property tax bills and the property tax bills of 1990, compare the figures.

If property values had increased at the rate of inflation, property tax bills would be $1,606. But housing prices have increased faster than inflation, so the median price the homeowner is paying is $1,875. That's a $269 difference per year, or a 17 percent increase after adjusting for inflation.

Ask students whether Springfield has had a tax increase. City officials will probably say no because the millage rate has remained at 18.75. But homeowners know that their tax bills are much higher. Can taxes go up without a tax increase? In this case, the answer is yes. The assessed value of the median-priced home has risen, so when all factors are considered, the city's tax revenues will rise along with the increase in the value of properties.

PART THREE: STORYTELLING

CHAPTER 7: THE INVERTED PYRAMID

Overview

This chapter is probably the most important of all those in the book. Students who have not mastered the basic skill of using inverted pyramid style in their writing will suffer throughout the rest of the semester. You may want to devote extra time to this chapter and draw up supplemental exercises that you can give to those students who are having trouble.

Some students will be impatient with the restrictions imposed by the inverted pyramid. However, good writing, in any style, flows from the discipline of the writer.

You may wish to have students analyze inverted pyramid leads from a local newspaper. If you have access to other newspapers or to the Internet, you can also ask them to compare different versions of the same stories.

We urge you to push students hard to make their leads clear and short. Too many of the examples they find in newspapers will be long and confusing.

At this point, be particularly conscious of students' tendency to put opinion, either their own or someone else's without attribution, into the story. When the reporter is chastised by his city editor for putting the phrase "careless smoker" into a lead without attribution, we are attempting to bring the point home with finesse, not a sledgehammer. But you may want to dwell on that point more during a lecture.

As in most of the chapters, the answers that follow are but one version of a correct answer. There are numerous possibilities.

Solutions to Textbook Questions and Exercises

1. Who: United Jewish Appeal
   What: sponsoring a walk-a-thon
   When: this morning
   Where: in Springfield; a more specific location would have to appear later
   Why: to raise money for The Soup Kitchen
   How: through a walk-a-thon, in which participants get pledges (That, of course, would have to be explained later in the story.)

2. Missing from "a" is how; from "b," why and how; from "c," how and who; and from "d," why. Therefore, "a" answers the most questions. However, we like "c" the best. It doesn't have as much information, but it is the easiest to understand, and it shows readers how the news affects them.

3. Options:
   a. The nation's funeral home directors are required to offer you detailed cost estimates because of a law effective today.
   b. You will have an easier time determining the cost of a funeral starting today.

c. A new disclosure law, going into effect today, will make it easier for you to determine the cost of a funeral.

Of these three, "b" is probably the best because it speaks clearly and directly to the readers' interests. The students will have to make the case for their own rewrites.

4. Forty miles from protesting peace activists, including 450 physicians, Tuesday the United States detonated a nuclear weapon with a yield equivalent to 150,000 tons of TNT.

The test was conducted 2,000 feet beneath the surface of Pahute Mesa in the Nevada desert, according to Department of Energy officials.

5. A 7-year-old boy missing for three years was found in New Jersey Monday night after a neighbor recognized the child's picture when it was shown after a television movie about a missing child.

(If the paper is in New Jersey, the lead would contain more specific information about the location. If the information about the find had already been broadcast, the newspaper would have led with the arrest.)

6. One hundred forty passengers were evacuated safely from a jet at the LaCrosse, Wis., Municipal Airport after a landing tower employee spotted smoke near the wheels Monday.

The smoke was caused when hydraulic fluids leaked onto hot landing brakes of Northwest Airlines Flight 428 from Minneapolis, according to Northwest spokesman Bob Gibbons.

7. Photographs: of the evacuation, of workers cleaning up the material around the plane after the evacuation, of workers towing the plane to the hangar.

Graphics: a cutaway of the airplane to show how passengers exited the plane; a drawing showing how the hydraulic fluid would leak onto the brakes.

8. You are on your own for this one. It's a good exercise, though, because it forces students to read a newspaper.

9. If you don't have access to the Internet, use printed newspapers. If at all possible, however, use of the Internet is preferable because this exercise can help students become more familiar with it at the same time they learn something about the inverted pyramid.

Solutions to Workbook Questions and Exercises

1. a. scientist
   b. says he will fight to be reinstated
   c. not answered
   d. New York (in dateline)
   e. Why he will try to be reinstated is not answered, but why he was dismissed is because of vigorous tobacco industry lobbying.
   f. not answered
   g. 1. Who?
      2. What?
2. a. Who: Springfield police
   b. What: arrested a local woman
   c. When: Thursday

d. Where: isn't indicated, although if this were in Springfield, the lack of a dateline indicates it is a local story
e. Why: for allegedly filing a false police report
f. How: not in lead
g. 1. Who?
   2. What?

3. Charging she filed a false report of a rape last month, Springfield police Thursday arrested a local woman.

4. a. Who: United Way Board of Directors
   b. What: will announce allocation plans
   c. When: at 2 p.m. tomorrow
   d. Where: at the board's offices
   e. Why: not answered
   f. How: not answered
   g. 1. Who?
      2. What?

5. a. President Michael Quinn
   b. agreed to reconsider his recommendation
   c. Friday
   d. Springfield University
   e. implied that it is because of the protest (The story would need evidence to support that.)
   f. not answered
   g. not stated in lead (Written for the campus paper, the "so-what" could be cheaper rates for students. Written for the local daily, it could be reduced revenues for the university.)

6. a. B and C each answers four of the six basic questions in the lead. Both leave "why" and "how" for later. The "where" is in the dateline.
   b. Other than the "where," which is first because it is in the dateline, the first question answered is:
      A. Who?
      B. Who?
      C. Who?
      D. What?
   c. D answers four of the six questions in a straightforward manner. A is probably a better teaser; C is an alternate approach that leaves the key information for the second and third paragraphs.

7. You can require two or more stories for comparison, but you'll usually find different versions of the same stories by using the Associated Press, Knight-Ridder News Service, *The New York Times*, *Los Angeles Times*, Gannett News Service and *Washington Post*.

8. a. All three answer four of the six questions. A omits "when" and "how"; B and C omit "why" and "how."
   b. Other than the "where," which is first because it is in the dateline, the first question answered in all three is "who."
   c. All three work; there is no "best" answer. A is a simple approach that includes "why" (inflation); B tells "when," which the others do not; and C translates the increase into $31, a meaningful figure to many readers.

d. If you are one of the nation's 40 million Social Security recipients, your check will go up 5.4 percent in January. The average increase is $31.

9. The faculty's proposal to adopt plus/minus grading could lower your grade point average. (Story would go on to show the difference in grade point average between an A and an A– or a B+.)

10. Beginning next semester, you can register by phone without even getting an adviser's approval first.
   Or:
   Beginning next semester, you can let your fingers do the walking at registration time.

11. *Note:* If your students included the name of the engineering company, make sure that they checked the city directory and used the correct name—Gross Co. Engineers.
    a. Duane LaChance, 55, a Springfield pipe fitter, suffered third-degree burns Tuesday in an electrical accident at the Springfield Municipal Power Plant, 222 Power Drive.
    b. A Springfield pipe fitter suffered third-degree burns Tuesday in an electrical accident at the Municipal Power Plant, 222 Power Drive.

12. a. James W. Cunning, 20, of 505 W. Stewart Rd., was injured late Saturday in a two-car accident on U.S. 63 just north of Blue Ridge Road.
    b. A Springfield man was injured late Saturday . . .

13. Comedian Chevy Chase was named yesterday to the Board of Trustees of Bard College, Annandale-on-Hudson in New York.

14. At least 15 people were killed and 175 were injured (date) in a collision between an Amtrak train and three Conrail locomotives near Chase, Md. The accident is the worst in Amtrak's history.

15. a. Throwing her support behind First Ward Council Member Hong Xiang, Mayor Juanita Williams said yesterday that she will not run for re-election.
       (The preceding lead anticipates broadcast coverage of the news conference and emphasizes the Xiang aspect in order to give the story a fresher angle. Less fresh would be: Mayor Juanita Williams said yesterday that she would not run for re-election. She announced at a press conference in Springfield City Hall that she would support First Ward Council Member Hong Xiang.)
    b. Who: Mayor Juanita Williams; what: said she would not run for re-election; where: would probably appear in the second paragraph in either approach; when: yesterday (day of week); how: not in the first example because it makes it too wordy, and it is not important enough. It can appear in the second paragraph.

16. a. The Springfield City Council will vote on a proposal to give members of the city employee Local 45 a 4 percent pay increase when it meets at 7 p.m. (day) at City Hall.
    b. The Springfield City Council will consider a noise ordinance (day) as a result of complaints from residents who live near fraternity and sorority houses.
       The council meets at 7 p.m. in City Hall . . .

17. a. The Springfield Board of Education Monday abolished restrictions on personal appearance and driving to school and toughened the drug policy. The new rules go into effect (date).

b. The Springfield Board of Education Monday night adopted a revised school manual that loosens restrictions on personal appearance and tightens rules on drug-related offenses.

c. The Springfield Board of Education Monday abolished restrictions on hair length, carrying cell phones and driving to school. It also decided that any student caught with drugs will be suspended for up to 20 days and turned over to juvenile authorities.

d. The Springfield Board of Education Monday revised its school manual to loosen restrictions on personal appearance and tighten rules on drug-related offenses. Board members also heard that negotiations with maintenance workers over a new contract are continuing and that school enrollment is up by 17.

e. You can let your hair grow, carry a cell phone and drive your car to school beginning (date). But if you get caught with drugs, you'll be suspended for up to 20 days and turned over to juvenile authorities, the Springfield Board of Education decided Monday.

18. a. The Republican candidate for mayor last night said he has not received any donations from Main Street merchants, but he refused to reveal the names of donors until after the election.

b. Mayoral candidate Jesse Abraham said last night he would widen and improve Main Street and buy land to build a city park. He also said he had not received any donations from merchants but declined to reveal the list of his donors until after the election.

19. Neighbors Gary Roets, 49, of 6204 Ridge Road, and Duane Craig, 51, of 6206 Ridge Road, met abruptly as they backed out of their driveways Tuesday morning. The untimely meeting caused about $650 in damage to their cars.

20. The last two paragraphs put the opening information in context and serve as the so-what factor for the story. This is not just a story about Terry Woolworth; it is a story about the larger debate.

21. The lead that answers the most questions isn't necessarily the best one. If long, confusing sentences result, the lead should be simplified. Writers must make decisions about which of the seven questions are appropriate for the lead.

22. A. Reordering the paragraphs: 4, 2, 3, 1, 6, 5.
    B. Reordering the paragraphs: 4, 3, 5, 6, 2, 1.

23. Michael Quinn, Springfield University president (avoid long titles in front of names; "president" is no longer capitalized), said today that he will recommend to the Board of Curators that tuition be increased by 6 percent (note use of the word rather than the symbol) each of the next two years.

    The Curators meet at 10 a.m. Friday (delete "morning") in (delete "room") 249 Student Union, 322 University Avenue.

    Milo Nishada, Springfield Student Association president (with the context, you *could* delete "Springfield" if you wish), said . . . (rest is correct).

24. A bank president and his wife, a local talk-show host, were killed Monday afternoon in a two-car collision at Ninth and Elm streets.

    James Westhaver, 55, president of Merchants National Bank, and his wife, Martha, 60, whose show was broadcast on KTGG television, were killed in the accident, which also injured two city employees.

    Prosecuting Attorney James Taylor said he would investigate whether involuntary manslaughter charges should be filed against the driver of the other car, James West, 43. Police already have filed charges of careless and imprudent driving against him.

West suffered a broken leg and possible concussion. His passenger, Samuel Blackwater, 32, had two broken arms and a broken nose. Both are employees of the city's Parks and Recreation Department.

Witnesses told police that the car driven by West ran a red light as it headed south on Ninth Street. Hit broadside, the Westhaver car rolled over three times and came to rest against a light pole.

Westhaver had been the bank's president since Jan. 1, 1973. He had been employed there for 33 years. He was treasurer of the Chamber of Commerce.

Funeral arrangements are incomplete.

25. a. Suggestions: Eliminate "three neighborhoods" and "200 items"; move down ages and addresses.

   b. Note that the lead should eliminate the suspects' names. Suggestion: Police arrested a man and a woman on burglary charges resulting from a spree of 14 break-ins netting $43,000 in stolen goods.

CHALLENGE EXERCISE

26. A. A fire believed to have been started by an arsonist killed 13 thoroughbreds housed in a barn at Lincoln Downs Race Track in Springfield today.

   An arson squad has been assembled. Fire Chief Bernard Perry said, "The fire exploded near the center of the barn. Flames were shooting out of the building when we got here."

   Dan Bucci, assistant general manager of the track, said the only heaters and electrical outlets were in the tack rooms at the ends of the one-story wooden structure.

   In addition to the thoroughbreds, two saddle horses died. Ten horses, including two who stampeded through the yard with their backs on fire, escaped.

   Albert Ramos, a jockey from Miami, Fla., watched as workers cleaned up the area.

   "Those are my best friends," he said, pointing to the surviving horses. "I love horses more than I do people. I feel like I want to cry."

   (Instructors: Either as part of the assignment or as part of the discussion after the story has been written, you may want to have the class list the questions that are unanswered on this fact sheet. For instance, how many of the 10 that escaped were thoroughbreds? Will the racing season be postponed? How long? Was the building insured? What was the dollar loss in horses and building?)

   B. A Springfield University student died (date) soon after a catamaran on which she and three fellow students were sailing capsized in the ocean near Daytona Beach. Her three companions reached safety after swimming for more than six hours to shore.

   Christy Wapniarski, 19, died as she was attempting to swim the four miles to Ormond Beach. Before she disappeared under the water, her companions heard her yelling that she had been attacked by a shark.

   One companion, Randy Cohen, 19, is in Halifax Hospital, where he is being treated for dozens of Portuguese man-of-war bites. The two others, Daniel Perrin, 20, and Tammy Ennis, were treated and released.

The four, who did not have life jackets, had spent the previous night clinging to their catamaran, which had capsized about 5 p.m. Saturday. At dawn, they began swimming for shore.

Interviewed in the hospital today, Cohen said he was about 20 feet ahead of Wapniarski when she yelled that a shark had attacked her. Ennis warned Cohen not to help.

"Randy, don't go back there; you'll get eaten, too," she said. Cohen went to Wapniarski anyway. When he arrived, she was unconscious, but he could see no sign of a shark. Perrin, who had been swimming behind Wapniarski, checked her pulse and told Cohen she was dead. Cohen towed her for about 15 minutes before he became exhausted and had to release her.

(Instructors: There is no age given for Ennis. Students often get the names wrong in this account.)

CHAPTER 8: WRITING TO BE READ

Overview

A former editor once said of a reporter who had won two Pulitzer Prizes, "He can report, but he can't write. And what's worse he doesn't know he can't write. He'll fight you for every word."

Surprising as it may be, many successful reporters have been saved from embarrassing themselves by rewrite persons and copy editors. But it is getting tougher than ever to break into the business without writing skills. In fact, some editors today are looking for outstanding writers in the belief that reporting skills can be taught on the job.

At least initially, most students are attracted to newspaper work because they like to write. Too many of them are not willing to learn the basics, and it is our experience that many high schools are failing to give students a solid foundation in grammar.

In this chapter, we reassert the importance of good writing and help the student to recognize the basic elements of good writing. To many journalists today, good writing begins and ends with the lead. But good writing is much more than that. Neither you nor we can teach students how to be good writers, but we can teach them the characteristics of good writing and give them an appreciation for it. And as journalists, we add the dimension of reporting, which makes good writing possible.

Solutions to Textbook Questions and Exercises

1. a. ensure   c. refuted
    b. annoying   d. mitigating
2. The entire passage, from a Pulitzer Prize-winning story in the *Philadelphia Inquirer*, is written in parallelism. We have italicized the most obvious repetitions.

    This assessment may prove overly optimistic. For perhaps in no other area of modern technology have *so many* experts in the government, industry and science been *so wrong so many times* over *so many* years as have those involved in radioactive waste.

They said, repeatedly, that radioactive waste could be handled like any other industrial refuse. *It cannot.*

They said that science had most of the answers, and was on the verge of getting the few it did not have, for dealing with radioactive waste permanently. *It did not, and it does not.*

They said that some of it could be buried in the ground, like garbage in a landfill, and that it would pose no health hazard because it would never move. *It moved.*

They said that liquid radioactive waste could be put in storage tanks, and that rigorous safety systems would immediately detect any leaks. *The tanks leaked for weeks and no one noticed.*

3. a. Place a comma after "system" because this is a compound sentence. Do not hyphenate "newly enacted" because you do not hyphenate "-ly" adverbs.
   b. Again, put a comma after "night" because this is a compound sentence. These two sentences illustrate how damaging a missing comma can be in compound sentences. In both cases, the reader would get far into the next clause before realizing the error.
   c. The sentence is correct. It has a compound predicate.
4. Break the information down to per capita figures. The student council's budget amounts to $18.42 ($18) per student. The city council's budget amounts to $42.86 ($43) per resident.

   Phrased another way, it costs each student $18.42 to support the student council. The city spends $42.86 to provide services to each resident.

   When dealing with the city figures, be sure to differentiate between residents and taxpayers. Each taxpayer contributes much more than $42.86.
5. One way to multiply the impact of this assignment is to make everyone's examples available to the entire class. In the process, you will acquire a wealth of examples.
6. If you have software that measures readability levels, you can use it on this assignment.
7. Most newspapers shoot far over the heads of what they consider their average reader. But *The New York Times* normally has a higher readability score than the Associated Press because of the different audiences.

Solutions to Workbook Questions and Exercises

1. a. effect
   b. Because
   c. torturous
   d. farther
   e. verbal
   f. air
   g. eluded
   h. fewer
   i. convinced
   j. concrete
   k. all right
   l. alluded
   m. bloc
   n. fliers
   o. from
   p. sewerage
   q. While
   r. disinterested
   s. sighted
   t. "demands" is correct because there is a threat—the strike

u. composed/comprises x. consul
v. continuously y. exhaustive
w. council z. eager

2. A recent amendment to the state labor relations law makes it the "most comprehensive and complicated" law in the country, a Milwaukee attorney told school officials in Springfield on Tuesday.

   John Brown of the Brown and Jones law firm was one of two speakers at an arbitration workshop for school board members and district administrators. It was sponsored by Cooperative Educational Services Agency District 12.

3. Jack and Jill went up the hill to fetch a pail of water.

4. a. The car, which he smashed just a block from his home, is in the garage. (Of course, substituting "that" for "which" and eliminating the commas would change the meaning of the sentence.)
   b. Tonight's lecture, which is in the student lounge, is about juvenile delinquency.
   c. Everyone stared at the woman in the low-cut gown who was dancing with the dean.
   d. My wife was annoyed with me because I spilled paint all over the carpet.
   e. He gave the sweater, which he won in track, to a friend.
   f. He was strangled in his bed.
   g. Cooking in a fireplace saves energy.
   h. In the second half, James Carver returned punts 35 and 16 yards. That set up touchdown drives of 41 and 28 yards to make the score 27-3.
   i. Jumping over a fence, he ripped his pants.
   j. The company said its earnings are down from last year.
   k. The owner and his wife are in the racing business. The owner trained the 8-year-old gelding.
   l. Sheriff Burton Stephan on Friday pled guilty to charges of second-degree sexual abuse of a child under the age of 4.
   m. Waiting patiently to begin drawing, the child sits in a high chair across the table.
   n. Tampa police shot and killed a man who they say pinned an officer between two cars Friday. It was the second fatal shooting of a suspect this week.

5. a. 20 percent
   b. 50 percent
   c. Why is the tuition rising at a much faster rate than the budget?

6. a. Sources of statistics; base year for increases and decreases (1996); definition of entertainment expenditures.
   b. Suggestion: Focus on the contrast between the increase in entertainment expenditures and the drop in alcohol expenditures.

7. This story has an opening, not a lead. The opening is a re-creation of a dream. The opening consists of the first five paragraphs. It ends with, "Sometimes, Jonathan wins."

   The sixth and seventh paragraphs make up the nut, or theme, paragraphs. They end ". . . about what transpired next aboard Southwest Airlines Flight 1763." You could have started a more traditional story with these two paragraphs.

   The final two paragraphs of this excerpt support the nut paragraph.

8. a. Compound. The structure sets two facts next to each other but does not explicitly establish the relationship.
    b. Complex. This structure establishes cause and effect most effectively.
    c. Two simple sentences. Like the compound sentence, it does not explicitly show the relationship.
9. The version the students are rewriting—and ruining—was written on deadline. Although it is choppy, an appropriate pace builds up to the action. When students are forced to reduce the number of sentences to about four, the pace is destroyed.
10. Once they found a dead man, and the desert all around him was ripped up as if he'd gone berserk. They could see marks on the ground where he'd crawled on his belly, swimming across the sand. Sometimes they find people with their shoes and clothes piled neatly beside them where they decided to lie down and peacefully die. When the body temperature soars, the brain seems to cook. People pitch off their clothes to escape the heat. They bury their heads in the sand, in the hope of cooling their craniums.
    But still they keep coming, day after day, night after night.
11. Word counts: 15, 13, 13, 15, 15, 17, 17, 14, 13, 12, 15, 17, 18, 19 and 19. There are 15 sentences of similar length, for 232 words. The following revised story has these word counts: 15, 10, 21, 8, 14, 17, 13, 10, 14, 15, 19, 7, 11 and 19. It has 14 sentences, totaling 193 words.

    Almost three times as many students as usual were absent from Shelton public schools Monday. It appears that a "flulike illness" may be to blame.

    Neither Sam Ford, city health director, nor John Simmons, Wisconsin's assistant director of epidemiology, is ready to declare a flu epidemic. Tests will not be complete for several weeks.

    Boone, Chippewa and Columbia counties have reported "widespread cases of flulike illness," Simmons said.

    The tests involve taking blood samples during and after a person's illness to isolate possible flu strains. The patient must recover before a final determination can be made, Simmons said.

    Positive identification of the flu virus has not been made. "It is quite evident that incidents of flulike illness have increased recently," Ford said. "Some of it is probably real flu, but we have no proof of that yet."

    Although Simmons said Monday that excessive absences have not been reported in the state, local schools reported 1,869 absences. The average ranges from 450 to 600.

    Simmons said the number of reported illnesses increased after the holidays. Holiday travel and increased contact with family and friends may be responsible for the number of illnesses, he said.

12. The answer depends on the student's response to exercise 11.
13. a. *Since 1949*, the federal government has quietly spent hundreds of millions of taxpayers' dollars building—and then abandoning—nearly a dozen pilot plants and experimental facilities to produce synthetic fuels.
    Time and again, the plants showed that it was possible to turn coal into synthetic crude oil or natural gas.

And time and again, the government and its contractors in private industry walked away from the plants, always stopping short of actual commercial production.

Now, under the Energy Security Act that became law in June, the government intends to distribute not just hundreds of millions, but billions of tax dollars to oil companies to construct yet more pilot synthetic fuel plants and experimental facilities to conduct yet more tests.

b. Here is how AP wrote the story:

The nation's largest teachers union issued a task force report today urging that public schools be "totally restructured" to meet the needs of tomorrow's students.

The report by the National Education Association's Blue Ribbon Task Force on Educational Excellence established a year ago consisted mainly of a lengthy laundry list of suggested educational reforms, including better teaching conditions and sharply higher starting salaries of $29,000 to attract better people into the profession.

The 18-page report, "An Open Letter to America on Schools, Students, and Tomorrow," was being released at a news conference in Minneapolis two days before the 1.6 million-member teachers union begins a four-day annual meeting on Sunday in that city.

NEA President Mary Hatwood Futrell said in the introduction to the report that "all the many national reports on education released so far have lacked one critically important element: the perspective of the men and women who teach and serve our nation's young people."

The report offers the union's hoped-for vision of schools in a lengthy section, "Education in the Year 2001." Education will start earlier, it said. New technology will enhance learning, but books, discussions, lab experiments, writing and lectures will still play major roles in learning. Adults will return to school and view learning as a lifelong activity.

Teachers themselves will be held "rigorously accountable," and "only the most talented will be allowed to teach."

c. Shaggy, suspendered and sporting a tatty aviator's cap with the earflaps lowered, George Ballis is a transplanted Minnesotan who moved to California's Central Valley in 1953.

Ballis has been asked barbed questions *ever since.* He lives in a rambling bungalow embraced by grapevines and orange trees, where he plots the latest assault on California's agribusiness establishment, or, as he prefers, "the biggies."

Depending on your point of view, *Ballis* is either a populist firebrand slugging it out for truth, justice and the American way, or he is simply a loud, misguided pain in the neck.

Either way, he is in the middle of the fierce and occasionally vicious skirmish over government water subsidies 20 miles west of Fresno in the Rhode Island-size Westlands Water District. Last year, the district's cotton, tomatoes, barley, wheat, cantaloupes and other crops were cashed in for more than a half billion dollars.

51

This cornucopia is made possible by the federally financed San Luis Unit, a reclamation project that began delivering rivers of water to *Westlands* in 1968. The project was designed to benefit small farmers—limiting water rights to 160 acres (320 acres for a married farming couple) with only a few exceptions.

However, according to government documents, roughly half of Westlands' half-million acres exceeds the acreage ceiling. *The entire district* is owned by about 250 landowners, including Southern Pacific Railroad, which holds 105,000 acres. *Other large landowners* include the Boston Ranch with 26,000 acres.

14. a. simile
    b. metaphor
    c. simile
    d. simile
    e. metaphor
15. a. At first it sounded like a lion roaring in a tin cup. Then the door snapped from its hinges and blew across the hall as if it had been punched in the stomach.
    b. like a scared screech owl . . .
    c. The children scrambled for the candy like ants after sugar.
    d. The only thing worse would be the smell of a thousand rotten eggs. The fish lay helter-skelter, one decomposing frame merging into another.
    e. like a pail of cold water on a hot face . . .
    f. issued a hoarse rowooooo
    g. exposing a family for what it used . . .
    h. glossy, like a pool ball with ridges . . .
16. The U.S. government debt would run the university for 21,930 years at current rates.
17. The smallest man on the wrestling team is a thumb shorter than the average seventh-grade boy. The wrestler can just see over (the star)'s belt buckle, eye to bellybutton.
18. The equipment you buy with your sewer and water fees is less likely to end up in employees' homes now that the Sewerage & Water Board has cracked down on employee theft.
19. A surgical technique to correct poor distance vision may also speed up the decline in your ability to see things close by.
    Researchers, who released the results of a 10-year study on the procedure, known as radial keratotomy, said on Wednesday that the side effect should be a consideration in deciding whether to have the operation.
20. The story is full of specific detail instead of generic statements. For instance, the backhoe fell off the truck's flatbed instead of falling off the truck. In addition, verbs such as "shorn" are more specific than "cut off." Boldface print identifies these details in the following version, which also avoids the passive voice found in the second paragraph of the original.

Two people died Thursday when a backhoe fell off a truck's **flatbed** and **sliced** the top off an oncoming vehicle near Fairchild Air Force Base.

The backhoe's **bucket** sheared the top off the **Suburban** at about **hood height.** The impact forced the front seats **backward** and tore off the **dashboard, roof and steering wheel.**

Parts of the car lay in a heap of **crumpled metal and glass** under the overpass. The **silver** Suburban was identifiable only by a **1983 owner's manual lying in the dirt nearby.**

Both victims wore seat belts, but in this case, that was irrelevant, Sale said. Both suffered head injuries.

Sleeping bags, a Coleman cooler and fishing equipment scattered on the highway and in the back of the Suburban suggested a camping trip. **Unopened** cans of **Pepsi** were jammed behind the front seat of the car.

21. A Springfield man, though burned on 50 percent of his body, is in satisfactory condition today after a one-car accident on Interstate 70, 20 miles west of Springfield.

    Gary Evenson, 33, told police he fell asleep at the wheel. His car hit a road construction barrier, left the road, rolled over three times and caught fire.

    A passing motorist pulled Evenson to safety.

    Besides the burns, Evenson suffered a broken arm and a slight concussion.

22. Gary Evenson was tired but excited. He was going to Kansas City to surprise his fiancée with the new green-and-white Pontiac Bonneville he had just purchased. They would use it on their honeymoon next weekend.

    Evenson, 33, had just finished his second week of 16-hour days in St. Louis and left immediately for Kansas City.

    He never made it.

    Twenty miles outside Springfield on Interstate 70, Evenson fell asleep at the wheel. His car hit 24 road construction barriers, left the road, rolled over three times and caught fire. A passing motorist pulled him to safety.

    Evenson suffered burns over 50 percent of his body. He also has a broken arm and a slight concussion, but he is in satisfactory condition at Springfield Hospital.

    His fiancée, Nancy Mohr, 33, of Lansing, Mich., said she didn't care about the car.

    "I'm just happy Gary is alive. We can always buy another car."

    Her fiancé did care.

    "I didn't even have insurance on the car," he said. "This is a terrible thing."

    Police ticketed him for careless and imprudent driving.

    The wedding has been postponed.

23. A DePere, Ill., woman has offered a $500 reward for the return of the family's dog.

    Marcelle Sosinski of 2990 W. Hanover St. said the dog, a German shepherd, had been sitting outside a restaurant Saturday evening at the Lincoln County fair in Springfield while the family was eating. When the family came out, the dog was gone.

24. A 12-year-old girl's German shepherd guide dog is missing, and the church that donated the dog is offering a $500 reward for its return.

Marcelle Sosinski of 2990 W. Hanover St., DePere, Ill., thinks the dog was stolen Saturday night while the family was eating at a restaurant at the county fair in Springfield.

"Duke wouldn't leave," Mrs. Sosinski said. "He was too well-trained. He loved Mary too much. He had to be stolen. He had to be tricked."

The Sosinskis slept in their car Saturday night and resumed their search Sunday morning.

Members of Sacred Heart Catholic Church in DePere raised $3,800 to buy and train the dog.

"We have to find that dog," Mrs. Sosinski said. "He's not just a guide dog; he's Mary's best friend."

25. The short sentences reflect the action being described. Notice, too, that the scene is written in the present tense to give it a sense of immediacy.

26. Two Springfield High School students, just weeks away from graduation, died early Saturday when their car collided with a tractor-trailer truck.

A third student is in serious condition.

Dead are Donna Neal, 18, of 34 Wayside Drive; and Angela Kane, 18, of 263 Blue Ridge Road. Colleen M. Stark, 17, of 534 Grand Ave., was seriously injured.

Police said the accident occurred about 1:30 a.m. when the car driven by Neal went out of control as it rounded a curve near 8301 E. Stadium Drive on the north side of the Truman Sports Complex. The car, which was heading east, slid into the westbound lane and struck the driver's side of the tractor-trailer. All three women were thrown from the car.

The driver of the truck was not injured.

27. **CHALLENGE EXERCISE.** Last fall Donna Neal had to select her favorite hymns as part of a class assignment on funerals. The 18-year-old Springfield High School senior chose "Be Not Afraid," "One Body, One Bread" and "On Eagle's Wings."

Saturday afternoon friends and school officials were arranging to sing those hymns in a memorial to Donna and a classmate who died in an early morning car wreck.

Donna and Angela Kane, 18, died in the collision with a tractor-trailer truck near the Truman Sports Complex. Another classmate, 17-year-old Colleen Stark, was seriously injured.

Donna had selected the hymns when she was asked to write her funeral ceremony for a class in death and dying. She also chose a gospel reading and described how she wanted to be remembered after death.

"She said, 'I want to be remembered as happy,'" said Brother Mike Martin of St. Regis Church, which is next to the high school. "That helped us pick out the songs and the readings.

"The saddest part of her funeral is the gospel reading," Brother Martin said. "It's about a widow asking Jesus to raise one of her children from the dead and bring it back to the family. Donna's mother is a widow and has 13 kids."

The Springfield High School community reacted with shock as word of the wreck spread Saturday.

"I came in to grab a cereal bowl about 8 o'clock," said Brother Sidney Edmond. "One of the brothers said, 'I've got some bad news for you.' It was instant denial. I started saying, 'No, no.'"

Throughout the day students came to the school and the brothers' residence looking for solace.

CHAPTER 9: BEYOND THE INVERTED PYRAMID

Overview

Chapter 9 replaces the traditional section on feature writing. The title and approach are different from traditional textbooks because we believe the story organizations discussed here apply to all stories, not just features. While the inverted pyramid remains the basic vehicle to convey news, alternative story organizations are being used more frequently. We also are dealing here not just with leads, which most textbooks use to differentiate features from news, but also with story organization.

In this chapter, students should learn to recognize alternative story organizations in newspapers. They also should learn how to write these types of stories. If students are having difficulty, ask them to write just the opening of several stories so that they can concentrate on the anecdote or scenic opening, the theme paragraph and the transition to the body of the story. Once these steps are mastered, students can then work on polishing their writing skills.

Solutions to Textbook Questions and Exercises

1. Often, students will choose the same scene. You may even assign them to write about such a scene or event that occurred in class. It is useful to read the stories aloud in class and compare them. Also, it is useful to read or distribute them to the class as an accuracy check.
2. Is the anecdote interesting and pertinent, and does the transition make the connection between the lead and the theme paragraph?
3. It is possible to delay the transition and theme paragraphs longer in a chronological approach, but the chronology should lead somewhere fast.
4. Students have a tendency to cut too wide a swath on this assignment. They need to focus on some experience. What they leave out is at least as important as what they include.
5. As the chapter indicates, there are service journalism aspects to almost any story. A city council advance? Pull out the time, date and place of the meeting. Perhaps you could also list the council members' names and e-mail addresses or phone numbers. More typical service journalism stories will range from how to use the Internet to how to save money for college. Encourage your students to be inventive about how the story is told. Is traditional text even needed? Will a graphic with copy blocks work better?
6. We specify *The Wall Street Journal* and *USA Today* in this question only because they are available everywhere and always have focus structure stories. *USA Today*'s cover pieces in each of the four sections generally use this organizational structure. You could change the assignment to include different sources, however.
7. You may want to specify that students should use first or third person, or that they should choose one or the other. But the person the story is written in is less important than its use of anecdotes, transitions, theme paragraphs and so-what paragraphs.

1. Getting examples of writing that reflect reporting with all the senses will be hard enough, but the important thing is to lead a discussion evaluating the examples. Ask students which of the senses were hardest to find. Get them to think about using them in their own reporting.

2. There are thousands of possibilities. Here is one example of each. If you have students do exercise 1, you will soon have an extensive file of your own.

   Sight: Under the new snow, the street posts looked as though they had Mickey Mouse ears.

   Sound: When the penalty flag dropped, the hometown fans roared in unison, like a pride of well-rehearsed lions.

   Smell: The food court smelled like ripe garbage.

   Touch: The baby's hair feels like strands of silk.

   Taste: The steak tastes like charcoal.

3. A. Focus. "Wong and thousands . . ." is the transition to the theme paragraph, which follows.

   B. Focus using scene re-creation. The transition is the first sentence in the theme paragraph: "Then the resort . . ."

   C. Focus using anecdotal opening. The transition, a weak one, is the introduction to the two paragraphs setting the theme: "Her story is the story . . ." The next paragraph is also part of the theme.

4. Answers will vary.

5. This is exposition. These are facts delivered with skill but, nonetheless, in expository style. There is no scene setting and no dialogue. The last sentence is a nice bit of foreshadowing. It's a good example of the power of expository writing.

6. This is narration. The writer has taken readers into the emergency room. Readers can watch and listen to the action as if they were watching it on a stage. The reporter is nowhere to be seen.

7. a. This is dialogue because the characters are talking to each other rather than to the reporter. The writer has added context so readers can see the scene.

   b. To get this dialogue, the reporter would have had to ask questions such as, "What did you say then?" and "Then what did the boy say?" If the reporter were not trying to reproduce dialogue, the questions would have been different: "What did you do then?" "What were you thinking?" Because the answers would have been different, the quotations would probably be different. It would look more like the following:

   Russell Oakley, an orthopedic surgeon, said the wound looked as though it was caused by an AK-47.

   "When I mentioned the AK-47, the boy surprised me by saying he thought it was an M-16," Oakley said. "I didn't know he was alert enough to hear me, let alone respond to me.

   "He told me he was scared and asked me if he was going to die," Oakley said.

8. The details and descriptive verbs carry the detail. They are noted in boldface:

Billy Ross Sims is **handcuffed and sweating.** Not an easy combination.

As perspiration **beads up** on his forehead, then **drips into his eyebrows,** Sims—afraid of losing his train of thought, his rant—**dips his head down** to clear away the sweat **by dragging his face across the lap of his white** prison overalls.

His head **darts back up,** and it's as though he never stopped talking. **Talking and grimacing, talking and sweating** . . .

Take out the details and use more pedestrian verbs, and you get something like the following:

As perspiration forms on his forehead, Sims—afraid of losing his train of thought, his rant—wipes the sweat off his face on his prison overalls.

He brings his head back up, and it's as though he never stopped talking . . .

9. Without saying it explicitly, the foreshadowing promises that a story about the death of the lover is coming. Presumably, the death is caused by an earthquake.

10. Unfortunately, your students may have trouble with this assignment, especially if they rely only on newspapers. You'll find it often in *The Wall Street Journal* and frequently in the *Washington Post,* the *Los Angeles Times,* the *Miami Herald* and other large papers. We restrict students to nonfiction stories because that is the kind of stories they are learning to write.

Ask students to hand in the examples with citations. That way you'll start compiling a collection of your own.

11. The so-what is the last paragraph of this excerpt. That's OK because the preceding paragraphs say the same thing less explicitly. The real so-what adds a key element: the experts' opinion. The so-what paragraph could also be the lead.

12. Again, have students submit the examples with citations so that you can compile a collection of them. The fact that students will probably have trouble finding examples illustrates how important it is for them to learn how to craft the so-what. You may need to extend the search to such papers as *The Wall Street Journal.*

13. You may want to tell students that they can add details to round out the scene or anecdote. They should take the story through the transition into the main story. Here is one approach:

Pete Stenhoff was a physically fit, 210-pound linebacker for Chula Vista High School when he planted his helmet in the chest of a ball carrier two years ago. He hasn't walked since. Medics that night rushed Stenhoff to the hospital, where he learned he had cracked vertebrae.

Stenhoff is one of 20,000 youths who are injured playing high school football each year. Like Stenhoff, nearly 2,400 are permanently disabled. But he is luckier than some; 13 youths died last year as a result of their injuries on the football field.

"I knew the risks involved when I decided to play football," Stenhoff says, "but I wish I would have known just how bad it could be."

14. Bill Klisch, a 51-year-old autoworker, walked slowly to the cadence of a muffled drum. With him were 49 other workers, their wives and children.

Klisch and 44,000 others who had been laid off from Chrysler will receive their last supplemental unemployment checks next week. Those checks have been providing them with 95 percent of what they would be earning at Chrysler. With the supplement nearly ended, the workers and their families staged a mock funeral on April 1 to draw attention to their problem.

"My wife is handicapped and she's supposed to have an operation," Klisch said. "Our medical coverage is running out. Tell me what I'm supposed to do."

Chrysler laid off the workers five months ago. After next week, they will have to live on state unemployment benefits. That doesn't please another marcher, Henry Westoff, 44.

"They'll give us our jobs back after we've lost everything," he said.

15. This is how United Press International began the story:

When Lillian Garland had a baby five years ago, she set off a legal battle with long-term repercussions for working mothers.

One of 55 million working women in this country, Garland went to court when her employer, California Federal Savings & Loan, refused to reinstate her at the end of her pregnancy leave.

The U.S. Supreme Court sided with Garland, voting 6-2 Tuesday to uphold a California law requiring employers to grant up to four months unpaid disability leave to pregnant workers and to guarantee a job for them when they return.

16. You can change the direction of this assignment or give students options about the theme. For instance, you might tell them to write a story about their most memorable high school experience or their most embarrassing moment in college.

17. This exercise can provide more examples for your collection as well as the basis for a class discussion. You might have students turn their anecdotes in before class so that you can copy them to hand out to other class members. Or you may wish to make transparencies. If you teach in a computer lab, you could have students type them into the system so that everyone can call them up, or you could show them on the screen from your computer.

18. To make it useful, you tell readers *what* is on the agenda and, to the extent you can find out, what the likely voting outcome will be. Identify the positions of the members of the council. To make it usable, tell readers *when* and *where* the meeting is. If possible, offer phone/fax/e-mail addresses for the council members so that readers can express their views before the vote. If there is a specific time on the agenda for public comment, publish that information.

The point of this question is to show that service journalism applies to hard news as well as to features. It also shows that a good advance already has most of this information. The presentation, however, would be different. The paper would probably use a pullout listing agenda, time, date and place or a list of council members and how to contact them.

19. This exercise works well as a team class discussion. You should get a variety of suggestions: a map with a route and sequence numbered from the dorm to pay fees, get student ID, register for classes, buy books and supplies, and so on. Another map showing recreation locations. A list of important telephone numbers. A list of the five most popular places to party. Ten ways to shortcut the bureaucracy. A first-person story about a student who has been through the horror. Be sure to get them thinking about formats—stories, lists, maps, graphics—as well as the content. Make them fit the content to the format.

20. **CHALLENGE EXERCISE.**   To re-create the scene, the writer uses present tense to give a sense of immediacy and to take the reader there while it is happening. He chooses to view the action from the spectators' section, the same place the readers would be if they were there. He reports with his senses; ask the students which of the five senses are evident in the reporting. (They won't find evidence of touch and taste.) He chooses telling detail to show, not tell. He uses dialogue, albeit in small amounts.

PART FOUR: BASIC STORIES

CHAPTER 10: OBITUARIES

Overview

The value of obituaries often is overlooked both in news rooms and journalism classrooms. Because the form of the standard obituary is rather rigid, many instructors find the obituary helpful in teaching the inverted pyramid and accuracy.

You may find it useful to scramble information from obituaries printed in your local newspaper. You can introduce errors in the spelling of names, ages, addresses and so forth. If the necessary telephone books and city directories are available, students can be expected to correct the information and put the story in proper form. When you return a student's copy, you can include a copy of the obituary as it was written by the newspaper.

Because many obituaries are phoned in, it is useful for students to be given the obituary information orally in class. Permit them to ask questions. This exercise usually will demonstrate how difficult it is to get information by word of mouth. The letters "b" and "d" and "p" and "t" sound alike. If you use names with these letters, some students probably will misspell them.

You may also arrange with your local newspaper to copy the contents of two or three biographical files. Distribute copies of the clips, along with information from a mortuary form. Ask students to write a news obituary.

Before students do the exercises and assignments at the end of the chapter and in the workbook, you may wish to create new dates for the deaths, visitations and funerals to reflect the time during which you are actually working on the exercises. Make sure students figure the age correctly with the new dates.

Solutions to Textbook Questions and Exercises

1. a. Missing are survivors, date and place of birth, cause of death, employment history, memberships and achievements.
   b. Missing are cause of death, age and birth date, local address, survivors and career information.
2. Some papers lead only with the news of the death. Such formula writing shouldn't be encouraged. One factor determining whether to lead with the death or the burial is the time of death relative to the paper's publication.

   If the death occurred in the late afternoon or evening before morning publication, it might be appropriate to lead with the death. If it happened earlier, it might be appropriate to lead with the burial.

   Martha Sattiewhite, former president of the Springfield High School senior class, will be buried on July 2, her (age) birthday. She was killed June 30 in a car accident. (Instructors: Even though the senior class position is at least two years old, it establishes the connection to and identification for Springfield residents.)

3. Start calling the officers of the Lions Club. In many cities, there are several chapters. If you can't find out who the officers are, call any member. You

might try asking around the news room. If no one in the news room is a member, look in the advertising and circulation departments. You won't have to search long before finding a Lions member. If all else fails, the city directory often lists the local civic organizations and where they meet. The chamber of commerce is another source for that type of information. Once you have located someone in the club, find out who knew him best and take it from there.
4. There is no right answer to the question. A reporter must weigh the family's desire for privacy against the public interest.
5. We suggest that you assign one national and one local figure. You might even wish to have students interview local people for advance obituaries.

Solutions to Workbook Questions and Exercises

1. a. The basic information missing is cause of death, age and date of birth, address of deceased and names of survivors. Beyond that, information should be obtained about the person's life: occupation, clubs, achievements and so on.
   b. Survivors, date and place of birth, employment history, memberships, achievements and cause of death.
   c. Cause of death, date of birth, address, place of funeral services and who is conducting them, burial information and more career information.
2. a. Funeral services for Jenelle Crookstein, (age), a former Springfield High School Student Council president, will be at 1 p.m. Wednesday at the First Methodist Church.
      Ms. Crookstein, daughter of Don and Jane Crookstein, died (date) in a skiing accident in Vail, Colo.
   b. Pearl Cornell, (age), an active volunteer in Springfield organizations for nearly four decades, died (date).
   c. Jackson Adams, who died watching the oldest of his three sons play basketball (date), will be buried (date).
      Alternative: Jackson Adams, (age), a widower with three sons, died while watching his eldest play basketball yesterday.
3. Instructors: You may elect to change the date of death to the current year after June 16. Students would then have to refigure the age. The age will change according to the time of year you give the assignment.
   a. Ronald H. Lache, (age), a retired Air Force lieutenant colonel, died June 16 at his home, 104 Alhambra Drive, Springfield.
      Lache moved to Springfield five years ago from Dayton, Ohio. He was a member of the Newman Center and the Rock Bridge Lions Club.
      Graveside services will be at 2 p.m. (date) at Jefferson Barracks National Cemetery, Springfield. The Rev. Michael Finney will officiate. There will be no visitation. Parker Funeral Service is handling arrangements.
      Lache's wife, the former Delores Carney, died March 7.
      He was born Nov. 3, 1943, in Philadelphia to Harry and Thelma Curry Lache. He is survived by his mother and his son, Ronald, both of Springfield; and three daughters, Barbara Ann Peck of Dayton; Patrice Louis Wylie of Indianapolis; and Cynthia Lache of San Mateo, Calif.

Questions: When did he retire? Get some information about his Air Force career. Was he active in the Newman Center and Lions Club? If so, what did he do? If he was active, there could be some comment from friends.

b. Raymond Lee Hope, who has been an area auto supply businessman since 1967, died June 17 in Springfield Hospital. He was (age).

Funeral services will be at 2 p.m. June 19 at Faith Baptist Church with the Rev. Eugene McCubbins officiating. Burial will be at Memorial Park Cemetery.

Visitation will be at the Restwell Funeral Home, 10th and Walnut Streets, from 7 to 9 p.m. June 18.

Hope, of 1060 College Ave., had been a salesman for Springfield Auto Supply for the last year.

He was born July 3, 1925, in Chicago to Virgil and Flossie Dissart Hope. After serving in the U.S. Army during World War II, he married Mary Alice Willett in 1946 in Chicago. The couple moved to Springfield the same year.

He is survived by his wife; his daughter, Mrs. John (Raycene) Bach, of Springfield; and his brother, Earl, of Chicago.

Questions: What is the address of his daughter? This obituary presumably is for the local Springfield paper. Most would run addresses of local people. Talk to his co-workers at the auto parts store. Where else did he work? Talk to some of the people he worked with.

c. Henry Higgins, (age), a former University of Illinois football player, was killed Friday night in a two-car collision at the corner of U.S. 63 and Route NN in rural Lincoln County.

Funeral services will be Tuesday at the Newman Center with Father Ralph Green officiating. Burial will be in the City Cemetery.

Born in Springfield, Sept. 24, 1972, Higgins was president of his Springfield High School senior class and earned letters for two years as a tight end on the University of Illinois football team.

He recently earned his real estate license and was associated with the firm of West and Haver.

He was a member of the Springfield Jaycees.

He is survived by his wife, Cloris, of 209 Fourth St.; his parents, Ralph and Amy Higgins of Columbia; a sister, Ruth, of Birmingham, Ala.; and a brother, Russell, of St. Louis.

Friends may call at the Restwell Funeral Home, 2560 Walnut St., from 7 to 10 p.m. Monday.

4. a. Call the personnel office of the mill. Find out who his department foreman was. The foreman could identify the deceased's friends among the co-workers. Any of those co-workers might be a source of information about other aspects of the man's life: his hobbies, interests, charities and so on.

b. The information obviously suggests that the youth died of cancer. The best people to call are the parents. Another source would be the clergy handling the funeral. He or she probably can give you enough information so that you know how to approach the family. The clergy might even make the contact for you.

   c. Call the funeral home and find out whom they are dealing with. Check the newspaper library. Talk to neighbors. In each instance, you are trying to find information about this person's life. You never know where the next front-page human-interest story will come from.

5. a. You are balancing the fact that the person was a private citizen against the fact that the person committed suicide on public property. The fact that apparently no one saw the suicide because it was at night makes it an even tougher judgment call. Whether or not you would print the cause of death in the obituary, we suggest that it should at least appear in the news story.

   b. In this case, the public interest probably outweighs the family's claim to privacy. The mayor was a public official.

   c. AIDS is still a taboo subject among many segments of society. And as long as society regards AIDS as a stigma, newspapers will have a difficult time reporting it. Society loses because it will continue to lack information about the pervasiveness of the disease and will continue to deny that people in the mainstream of society can contract it. In this instance, most newspapers probably would not report the cause of death unless the family acknowledged it and permitted it to be made public. However, if the fact was confirmed, there would be no legal reason to withhold the information.

6. **CHALLENGE EXERCISE.** We suggest you assign one or two people, preferably one national and one local. You might even wish to have students do interviews with local people or faculty members for advance obituaries.

CHAPTER 11: NEWS RELEASES

Overview

This chapter comes early in the series on basic types of stories for two important reasons. First, it deals further with the question of news values. Students must recognize that material in a news release usually is self-serving to the person or institution issuing it. Second, news releases often are given to the beginning reporter to check out and to rewrite.

The chapter does not attempt to teach the student all there is to know about how to write a news release. That is not within the purview of this book. However, by taking a news course, a student who wishes to pursue a career in public relations will learn a great deal about the news release in these pages. It is essential for every journalism student to know the difference between a news story and a news release.

As you can see in the examples, the stress here is on checking and investigating further to develop a story with information that goes beyond what is in the news release. By emphasizing the need to do this, you are developing invaluable habits.

The chapter attempts to describe various kinds of news releases. We believe that students who become adept at recognizing them will know better how to deal with news releases.

Solutions to Textbook Questions and Exercises

1. The first part of the exercise, noting the departures from Associated Press style rules, is obvious. Note especially the problems the releases have with numbers and abbreviations. Let's look at each release to answer the other two parts of the exercise.

   Knowing what questions to ask about a story is half of rewriting it. Obviously, a large metropolitan newspaper would not have much room for news stories coming from these releases. However, the exercise here presumes that there is some room for the story if it has a strong local emphasis. Tell students to assume that the releases are from their community. A major purpose of the exercise is to teach students how to ferret out a story from a news release. Again, class discussion is most important. What you want is this reaction from students: "Why didn't I think of that?"

   a. This is an announcement release.

      The first question is: What are the Sheep Knowledge awards? Then: Who sponsors them? Are any local people likely to be interested? Will any enter? Where in Springfield will the test be given?

   b. This release announces and promotes.

      Are local people entering the flower show? What must one do to enter? Have any local people won in the past? Does the show welcome photographers?

   c. This is primarily an image-building release.

      What role, if any, will the students play in this new five-year plan? Will parents be involved? When might we see some actual changes taking place in the curriculum? Does "expansion" mean possibly enlarging the physical facilities?

2. We suggest that you allow students a set amount of time to read the releases and to prepare questions. Then you can serve as the source who answers any questions they might have. This means, of course, that you must study the release and be ready for logical, coherent answers. At times you may wish to be evasive, or perhaps even make an error or contradictory statement. You may want to lead the student to other sources. You may wish to take the role of the source.

   To be sure that you remember what you said, you may want to record your answers.

   You may also wish to ignore these particular releases and use some from your local newspaper office.

Solutions to Workbook Questions and Exercises

1. See exercise 1 above.

   a. This is an announcement release.

      The biggest question is: Just how important an honor is this? Then: How many men are named each year? Do they receive anything for being nominated? Is the only honor here a chance to buy a book with one's name in it? Does the local Jaycee organization endorse and cooperate with this awards program?

      After determining the worth of the award, you may want to contact the local people who received it. How do they feel about it? What

64

do they do? How did they get nominated? These questions may lead to other profiles and feature stories.
b. This is a release promoting a cause.

How long has Springfield University been running this program? With what success? What is Springfield's minority enrollment program? Has the university ever been in trouble over affirmative action programs? Has it lost government funding?

Can you find the names of some current Springfield students who went through previous programs? Do they credit the program as the reason they came to Springfield?

You may even wish to contact some of the students from the high schools who are coming to the program. And, of course, you want to mark your calendar to do a story when the program takes place.
c. This release is an announcement of an upcoming event.

The most obvious question is: What is the subject of Ackers' speech? Then: Is a copy of the speech available? How long will he talk? How many and what kinds of people will attend? Is it open to the public? To reporters?

Who will receive the "Outstanding Citizen Award"? Why?

Which officers and board members will be retiring? Why are they retiring?

What is the Woodhaven Bell Choir? Do they perform often? Are they worth a possible feature story?
d. This is an announcement release.

Must you excel at passing, shooting and dribbling to win a plaque? Do boys and girls compete in the same age grouping? In other words, do the girls compete with the boys? Do contestants compete by themselves, or are they placed on teams? Who will be doing the judging? Is this the first time the contest has been held?
2. See exercise 2 on page 64.
3. Journalists should not ignore news releases because they often generate worthwhile and important new stories. You might make a list of all the story ideas that the class came up with from the following news releases. Here are a few suggestions:
a. Check with some local farmers to see what use they are making of telecommunications. Find out what computer services are available to farmers and at what prices. Look for a possible success story about a farmer who increased profits greatly because of a computer network.
b. Interview administrators, teachers and students at several junior high schools or middle schools to find out how prevalent smoking is among teenagers. Try especially to find out where the teenagers are purchasing the cigarettes. You might consider an article on how people feel about First Amendment rights to advertise cigarettes.
c. Using local grocery stores as your primary source, investigate whether people are buying healthier foods. Check with the meat department to see whether sales of red meat are down, and with the seafood and produce departments to determine whether sales of these foods have increased.

You might also conduct a survey of what shoppers think is healthiest—"prime," "choice" or "standard" beef cuts.

d. Check local newspapers and radio and television stations and talk to reporters who cover trials and the courts. You may want to do a story on how the media handled a recent trial or some trial in your community. Ask the questions this release asks. Check with experts in the university law school and in your journalism school.

4. a. An independent organization (National Federation of Egg Carton Producers?) probably could confirm Zerbe's claim of being the nation's leading producer and the size of its lead over the number two producer. Check with the county to confirm that Zerbe is the largest employer.

 b. Suggestions: Move up the fact that Zerbe is the county's largest employer; eliminate the paraphrase from the company president; round off the number of cartons to 14.5 million.

5. **CHALLENGE EXERCISE.**   We chose these releases because they are relatively timeless and tied to no location. They provide an excellent means for teaching beginning reporters how to dig for good local stories with news releases as a starting point.

CHAPTER 12: SPEECHES, NEWS CONFERENCES AND MEETINGS

Overview

You may want to spend a good deal of time on this chapter. The subject matter lends itself well to events that students can attend and write about. For that reason the final exercise of the chapter instructs students to cover a speech, a news conference and a meeting. You may want to expand the assignment to include two or three of each.

We have divided the subject matter into three parts:

1. Preparing to cover speeches, news conferences and meetings.
2. Covering them.
3. Structuring and writing the stories.

Obviously, all three parts are important. But particular stress must be placed on preparation. This part of reporting is too easily skipped.

In the section on covering these events, you might want to spend a good deal of time on the matter of tape recorders. You cannot take for granted that students know how to use them or that they know their advantages and disadvantages. Certainly it is not universally true that tape recorders scare people or that they make people clam up. Besides, this argument is simply inapplicable when covering speeches, news conferences and meetings.

In the section on structuring and writing these stories, we stress the need for good quotes but warn against the quotation lead. Beginning reporters often are tempted to put the striking quote in the lead, even though that quote may have little to do with the rest of the story.

You also need to stress the final two paragraphs of this chapter. Students should use their imaginations and write well, even for these bread-and-butter stories.

1. You may very well wish to use a different public figure for this exercise and for the following one. Most important is that students know what source books and data banks could and should be used to gain background information.

   A library may have the following sources: *Biography Index, Current Biography, Dictionary of American Biography, Facts on File, New York Times Index, Readers' Guide to Periodical Literature, Webster's Biographical Dictionary, Who's Who, Who's Who in America, The International Who's Who.*

   We suggest also that you use the Dialog Database Search (Dialog Information Retrieval Service). Check these files: Biographical Master Index, Marquis Who's Who, National Newspaper Index, Magazine Index and Newsearch.

   Here is some of the background information a reporter would need to write a story about Sam Donaldson's appearance:

   > Donaldson was born in El Paso, Texas.
   > He holds a bachelor's degree from Texas Western College and did graduate work at the University of Southern California.
   > He began his broadcast career in Dallas in 1959, moved to WTOP Washington shortly thereafter and joined ABC News in 1967.
   > In 1998, Donaldson received the Broadcaster of the Year award from the National Press Foundation.
   > The *Washington Journalism Review* named him Best Television White House Correspondent in 1985. He was named best correspondent in the business in 1986, 1987, 1988 and 1989.
   > He has won three Emmys and a Peabody.
   > Donaldson currently is anchor of SamDonaldson@ABCNEWS.com, co-anchor of *20/20* and co-anchor of *This Week With Sam Donaldson and Cokie Roberts.*

2. Here's some of the required background information about Robert Redford:

   > Born Aug. 18, 1937.
   > Attended University of Colorado, the Pratt Institute in New York and the American Academy of Dramatic Arts in New York.
   > Won Academy Award in 1981.
   > Married Sept. 12, 1958; three children.
   > Redford founded the Sundance Institute and has become more and more involved in environmental issues. He is a strong supporter of the Natural Resources Defense Council, the Environmental Defense Fund and the National Wildlife Federation.
   > In 1989, he won a medal from the Audubon Society.

3. You may wish to assign several different meetings to different students. You might have a problem if you send out a whole class to bother the same people. You would expect the students to obtain an agenda and to prepare for it by getting background information on each item.

4. Here's a suggested lead and direction for the story:

   > Mexican President Vicente Fox told a regional economic and development group today that Mexico has rebounded from its financial

crisis of the late 1990s and now has one of the most stable economies in the world.

Fox told delegates to a meeting of the Organization for Economic Cooperation and Development that strict fiscal discipline led to the Mexican turnaround.

"In Mexico . . . we have learned that the fight for economic stability starts with an unbending and strict fiscal discipline," Fox said. He noted that Mexico has the highest reserves in its history and that the country's foreign debt is steadily declining. . . .

5. You may wish to send two or three students to each speech, news conference or meeting. That way you will be able to compare stories in their coverage of the event and the content. Making students find the story in the local newspaper accomplishes two things: It demonstrates how the students compare with the professionals, and it makes students read newspapers.

Solutions to Workbook Questions and Exercises

1. Here's some information on Toni Morrison:

Born in Lorain, Ohio, in 1931, and christened Chloe Anthony Wofford.
Poor, close-knit family, grew up in the Great Depression of the 1930s.
Entered Howard University, interested in theater, joined drama group.
Received M.A. in English from Cornell University in 1955.
Taught at Texas Southern University from 1955-1957, at Howard University from 1957-1964.
While at Howard, married Harold Morrison, a Jamaican architect; had two children; divorced in 1964.
After leaving teaching, worked as an editor at Random House.
First novel, *The Bluest Eye* (1970)—an expansion of a short story—was an immediate success.
Followed by *Sula* (1974), *Song of Solomon* (1977), *Tar Baby* (1981), *Beloved* (1987), *Jazz* (1992), *Playing in the Dark* (1992), *Race-ing Justice, EnGendering Power* (Editor, 1992), *The Nobel Lecture in Literature* (1994), *Birth of a Nation'hood* (Co-editor with Claudia Brodsky Lacour, 1996), *The Dancing Mind* (1996), *Paradise* (1998).
Won Pulitzer Prize for *Beloved* in 1988.
Won the Nobel Prize in literature in 1993.

2. Here's some information on Interior Secretary Gale Norton.

Born in Wichita, Kan.
Attended University of Denver; B.A. in 1975 and J.D. in 1978.
Norton previously worked with James Watt's Mountain States Legal Foundation and followed him to the U.S. Department of the Interior under the Reagan administration.
She is a proponent of oil drilling in Alaska's Arctic National Wildlife Refuge.
She served as Attorney General of Colorado from 1991 to 1999.
Norton is best-known for prosecuting tobacco companies and defending Colorado's anti-gay Amendment 2.
Married to her second husband; no children.

3. You may wish to assign several different meetings to different students. (You might have a problem if you send a dozen or more students to bother the same people for a class assignment.) You would expect the students to obtain an agenda and to prepare for the meeting by getting background information on each item. They will also need to know some background on people on the council. Perhaps the morgues or libraries of local papers would allow your students access. The students could speak to key people on each issue. Much of this depends, of course, on the size of your city or community.

4. a. We think it is important for students to read newspapers regularly—at least their local newspaper. Making them find a speech story forces them to do that. However, in order to make comparisons, you may want to assign a particular story. Of course, you also want students to attend the speech and then see how it was covered.

   b. Do the same for a story about a news conference.

   c. Do the same for a story about a meeting.

5. It is important that there be at least two versions so that students can compare and evaluate them.

6. Obviously, there is no *one* way to cover the content of these speeches. The lead, the approach, the structure of the stories will vary widely depending on the person writing the story, the locality and the size of the paper. For these stories we suggest one possible lead as well as the direction the story might take.

   a. Lead: Taking a cue from a magazine article she had read, Martha Saunders told graduating seniors at the University of West Florida that the most influential messages in our language often come in three-word phrases.

   Saunders, an assistant professor of public relations at the university, said she agreed with the article's premise that phrases such as "I love you," "There's no charge" and "And in conclusion" were phrases with impact.

   But she also added her own:
   "I'll be there."
   "Maybe you're right."
   "Your heart knows."

   The article would then comment on the three phrases with appropriate quotes and paraphrases.

   b. Lead: Moses came down from the mountain yesterday and delivered another decalogue.

   This time he came in the form of Fraser Seitel, senior counselor of Burson-Marsteller, and he spoke to the Cincinnati Chapter of the Public Relations Society of America. Seitel's 10 commandments were for those who work in corporate communications.

   Seitel's first commandment of public relations was "to hold as our one and only God the spirit of Truthful Communications." Seitel demanded disclosure rather than withholding. Communicators must not only explain what their organizations are doing but why they are doing these things.

The story would then pick other significant commandments with significant quotes. It might end as follows:

Seitel, who began his speech saying that the potential of the practice of public relations had never been brighter, concluded by saying he was convinced that "the halcyon days for this field lie just ahead."

c. Lead: A world-renowned journalism scholar has said he believes segments of American journalism and future journalists follow the pragmatic principles of Machiavelli.

John Merrill, emeritus professor of journalism at the University of Missouri, quoted journalist Robert Sherrill as the basis for a study he did with journalism students at Louisiana State University.

Sherrill wrote: "So long as reporters, vastly outnumbered and outgunned, are expected to penetrate these hostile areas [government and corporations] to obtain useful information, they can, I think, be forgiven for using almost any device or tactic so long as it enables them to bring back the bacon."

To his surprise, Merrill found that 66 out of 74 journalism students expressed agreement with Sherrill.

The article would then proceed to quote and paraphrase certain students' remarks.

7. News conferences are difficult to report because of the diversity of reporters' questions. The first one here is the easiest because it focuses on the resignation of the head of the journalism school. The news conference of the mayor in exercise 8 is more complicated. Pay special attention to what students choose for their leads. Encourage lists of important elements, and suggest a sidebar or two. You might consider the following:

Lead: The head of the university's journalism department announced her resignation today and cited inadequate funding for the program as her reason.

Jessica Jergens, who has headed the program for five years, told a group of reporters: "It has been no secret that I have had some serious differences with the administration of this university over how the journalism program continues to be funded. The faculty in journalism are too few and too poorly paid. The facilities are pathetic by anyone's standards."

Although Jergens said her proudest achievement was that the journalism curriculum is stronger and the faculty stronger as well, the goals of her "five-year plan" had not been met.

Jergens said that her resignation might please some in administration, but she denied that she had been asked to resign.

Better writing classes are what the school needs the most, Jergens said. That demands quality professors and small classes. "The biggest complaint in any area of professional journalism is that we are not turning out good writers," Jergens said. "Everything begins and ends with writing."

Jergens said she hopes to remain a teacher, but for the time being, she will shun administration.

8.   Lead: Mayor James Alton called for a stronger crackdown on drunken driving yesterday, saying he will continue to push for a tougher ordinance on first- and second-time offenders.
Alton's ordinance would put:

1. first offenders in jail for a night and revoke their licenses for 90 days;
2. second offenders in jail for 30 days and revoke their licenses for one year;
3. third and more frequent offenders in jail for six months and revoke their licenses for five years.

"Drunk driving kills," Alton said. "If someone drives while intoxicated, that person is a potential killer, a threat to every citizen."

In other matters, the mayor said:

- the crowded jail is a disgrace to the community;
- the police chief's son received a light sentence for driving with a revoked license;
- school bus accidents are more likely to be caused by inexperienced bus drivers who are hired by the school district because they work cheap;
- he would have had to ask Gerald Nicklaus to resign had he persisted on closed meetings for the Springfield Tomorrow Committee.

Regarding the resignation of Nicklaus, Alton said he was sorry that Nicklaus felt the way he did about the pettiness of the press. "Any public position demands that we put up with you people," Alton said.

9. **CHALLENGE EXERCISE.** This is an excellent exercise that will demonstrate to students how different professionals handle the same speech or press conference differently. It also makes students read newspapers.

CHAPTER 13: OTHER TYPES OF BASIC STORIES

Crime Stories Reporting Overview

Most young reporters can expect to cover crimes, accidents, fires and court news early in their careers. These types of stories, which test reporters' fact-gathering skills, are often assigned to beginners.

This section emphasizes the reporting and writing of crime news from the perspective of a general-assignment reporter, not simply the reporter on the police or court beat. Beat reporting is the focus of Chapter 14. We suggest that you emphasize the importance of having a good understanding of libel law when writing about crime. Since the potential for libel is so great in this type of reporting, you may want to consider assigning Chapter 22, Media Law, before or together with this chapter.

This chapter also provides an excellent opportunity for you to add variety to classroom sessions by inviting guest speakers. You may want to arrange for the local police chief, a police officer or a detective to visit the class.

71

Accident and Fire Stories Overview

This chapter includes a section on what to do at the scene of an accident, fire or disaster. It gives tips on what questions to ask and, perhaps most important, whom to contact. Another section emphasizes follow-up action and lists typical examples of how reporters are able to obtain the maximum amount of information. The emphasis throughout is on reporting rather than writing, but examples of various types of stories help to illustrate the points covered.

When students write their stories, emphasize the importance of getting names and addresses correct, getting the facts straight and improving the quality of the story with a human-interest element. All the basics of good reporting can be built into a well-constructed exercise on accident, fire and disaster coverage.

We have deliberately avoided the issue of a major disaster, such as an airplane crash with hundreds of fatalities. Reporting of such events likely will involve a team of reporters rather than a single individual, and your students probably are not ready to handle the massive amount of information that could be thrown at them in such an exercise. Keep it simple and emphasize the importance of detail.

Court Stories Reporting Overview

The section on court news gives an overview of how the court system operates. This knowledge is important to the reporter assigned to cover a court proceeding or to write about a case as it progresses through the court system. We have tried to take into account most of the quirks of state law, but undoubtedly some states have unusual procedures. You may want to discuss these differences with your students.

Again, you may want to consider inviting a guest speaker, such as a judge or a prosecutor, to visit the class during your discussion of this material.

Solutions to Textbook Questions and Exercises

1. It is useful to have students think about sources of information. This exercise is easy to complete and is not time-consuming. It requires students to think about possible sources.
2. In every city, the fire department will have policies about things such as who is allowed to talk with reporters at the scene of a fire and how close reporters may get to fire lines. An understanding of these policies can help the time-strapped reporter at the scene of a fire. If it is impractical to have each student contact a firefighter, try to have a representative of the fire department visit your class.
3. Federal officials or agencies that may help in accident, fire and disaster coverage (there may be many others):
   a. U.S. marshals
   b. U.S. courts
   c. U.S. attorney
   d. Federal Bureau of Investigation
   e. Bureau of Alcohol, Tobacco and Firearms

f. Federal Emergency Management Agency
g. U.S. Coast Guard and military officials
h. U.S. Department of Agriculture (flood and fire damage to crops)
i. Federal Aviation Administration
j. National Transportation Safety Board
k. U.S. Department of Homeland Security

4. Unless your municipal court is located so far away from the campus as to be inaccessible, it is a good idea to use this exercise. Any time students get out of the classroom and into a realistic setting, their reporting skills are greatly enhanced. If you can arrange with the judge or city attorney to meet with the class afterward and discuss the experience, the exercise will prove exceptionally valuable. This may not be easy to arrange, but it's worth the effort.

5. This exercise is simple to complete. Of course, the solutions will depend on the nature of the story the student selects. We find that letting the student choose the story, rather than selecting one for the whole class, works best. Some of the stories will be more interesting than others, and you can discuss the more interesting ones with the entire class.

Solutions to Workbook Questions and Exercises: Crime Stories Reporting

1. Here is one way to write the story:

A police officer arrived at the scene of a liquor store robbery (Monday) in time to fire a shot at the fleeing robber, but the man escaped.

Officer Anne Fulgham and her partner, Jose Lopez, arrived at the Black Derby Liquor Store, 2311 Ripley Way, in time to see the robber dart into an alley. The two officers followed, and after Fulgham shouted a warning she fired at the robber. She missed and he escaped.

A witness, John Paul Reinicke, 35, of 109 Ninth St., Apt. 3C, said he was walking down Ripley Way when the incident occurred. "The officers did a great job," he said. "The guy ran so fast he looked like a track star."

The alarm was triggered by Seve Bellinos, 28, of 4673 Bellinghausen Court. Bellinos told police the robber entered the store at about 7:12 p.m. with a pillowcase over his head. The man pulled out a pistol and demanded money. Bellinos was able to trigger the silent alarm, and Fulgham and Lopez arrived within three minutes.

Bellinos described the robber as a man about 6 feet tall and weighing 155 pounds. He was wearing blue jeans and a dirty white T-shirt with a torn right sleeve.

The owner of the store, Ralph Martinson, 53, of 109 Lincoln Terrace, said about $2,845 was taken.

Police Chief Antonio Grasso said a routine investigation of the incident will be conducted by the Internal Security Squad. Such investigations are conducted each time an officer fires a service revolver.

2. The rape victim should not be identified in the following story. Here is one way to write it:

A 19-year-old college student told police (Monday) that she was raped (Sunday) night near the Chemistry Building on the college campus.

The victim said the attack occurred as she was walking back to her dormitory room after going to a movie downtown. A man with a stocking mask displayed a knife and forced her into an alley beside the building, she said. He threatened to kill her if she screamed.

The rape was the 16th reported to police this year and the fourth in the campus area during the last six months.

The victim said her attacker was about 6 feet 4 inches tall, weighed about 210 pounds, had blond hair and blue eyes, and appeared to be athletic. Two of the earlier victims of campus-area rapes gave similar descriptions of their attackers.

The 16 reported rapes this year compare with two for the same period last year, and Police Chief Antonio Grasso said he plans to form a task force to deal with the problem. It will be composed of police, rape crisis center officials and others.

In addition, college officials said they will install emergency telephone lines around the campus and review street lighting in the area.

3. The three sources are:
   a. Police officials and their reports. From these sources you can get most of the information you need, including an outline of what happened and the details of who was involved.
   b. The victim or victims. A firsthand account is valuable for detail and quotations.
   c. A witness or witnesses. More detail and quotations, particularly if the victim is unavailable.
4. The top-ranking police officer and FBI agent should be contacted immediately to supply as much information as possible about the robbery. Next a reporter would look for the bank manager or the teller who was confronted by the robber. Then the reporter would try to find witnesses.
5. You may want to obtain this information yourself and give it to students to avoid a run on the police department. Most departments are happy to provide such information and have it readily available. This type of story is standard fare for newspapers.
6. a. Suggestion: Emphasize that although murders rose dramatically (from one to seven), violent crime overall fell 8 percent from 1993 (from 435 to 400).

   b.

	2002	2003
Murders	1	7
Rapes	35	27
Robberies	97	86
Assaults	302	280
All violent crime	435	400
Burglaries	576	603
Larcenies	3,404	3,420
Auto theft	172	172
All nonviolent crime	4,152	4,195

7. There probably will be both fire and police officials at the scene. Fire officials most likely will be attempting to recover the body by dragging the river or sending divers into it. Police officials will be responsible for securing the area from bystanders and press. Try to talk with the highest-ranking official of each agency. It's also possible that you will be able to locate a relative of the person believed drowned. That could provide a useful (though perhaps awkward) interview.

8. Tornadoes, hurricanes and earthquakes typically cause damage of such a magnitude that no early estimate is reliable. An insurance executive may be better able to estimate than a fire or police official. Readers should be informed in the story that the estimate is, at best, a guess.

9. Typically, the Red Cross, Salvation Army and similar agencies provide such relief help. Your editor should know which agencies handle such duties in your community.

10. There is little question about what the lead for this story should be. Essential elements are the death of the car's driver and the fact that his car collided with an empty school bus. Here is a possible version of the story:

> A 16-year-old (Springfield) man was killed this morning when his car collided with an empty school bus at Thompson Lane and Lindbergh Avenue.
>
> Kelvin L. Bowen of 513 Maple Lane died at 7 p.m. at Springfield Hospital, where he had been taken following the accident. He was the son of Mr. and Mrs. Lawrence K. Bowen.
>
> A passenger in Bowen's car, Brad Levitt, 16, of 208 Maple Lane, was injured. He is in satisfactory condition at the hospital. Also injured was Ruth L. Anderson, 42, of 88 Jefferson Drive. She was hurt after Bowen's car and the school bus collided and Bowen's car skidded into hers.
>
> Police said the accident occurred as Bowen attempted to turn left from Thompson Lane onto Lindbergh Avenue. He turned into the path of the school bus, which was headed north on Lindbergh. The bus, driven by Lindell B. Johnson, 24, of 3033 Jellison St., struck the left side of Bowen's car.
>
> Bowen's car crossed into the southbound lane and traveled 54 feet north of the intersection, where Bowen's car struck Ms. Anderson's, which was southbound on Lindbergh. Her car was forced off the road and into a ditch, police said.
>
> Police said Bowen's car was destroyed. They estimated damage to the bus at $1,000 and damage to Ms. Anderson's car at $250.

11. This exercise can be an excellent one if you prepare for it well. It encourages students to look for fresh angles to the story, thereby reinforcing the importance of doing more than simply rewriting an accident report.

12. Here is one way to write the story:

> An electrical short apparently started a two-alarm fire that caused $1.2 million in damage to an electronics firm Wednesday night.

Fire Lt. Stephen Gorman said the fire at T&L Electronics Co., 4404 U.S. 90, was reported at 9:23 p.m. by the company's night watchman. The watchman, Fernando Lopez, 27, of 209 E. Watson Place, said he was making his rounds when he noticed that the rear of the building was unusually hot.

"Then I turned the corner and saw flames leaping out from a room that contains the electrical circuit breakers, the water heaters and that type of stuff," Lopez said. "By the time I got to the phone, the whole back part of the building was on fire."

Lopez said the fire spread rapidly.

The first fire units arrived only four minutes after the fire was reported, Gorman said, and a second alarm was issued at 9:42 p.m. Eight fire vehicles and 45 men fought the blaze, which was reported under control at 10:56 p.m.

Capt. Anne Gonzalez, city fire marshal, said early indications are that an electrical short caused the fire. An investigation is underway.

Gorman said low water pressure in the area hampered firefighters. New water mains are to be installed in the area next year.

The business is owned by George Popandreau, who is on vacation in Florida. Popandreau, reached by phone, said the building and contents are fully insured. He said he will return to the city tomorrow to begin moving the business to another location and to restock the inventory.

13. Be careful about including the information about Stone being drunk. That is not proven, and it could be libelous. Here is one way to write the story:

Two (Springfield) residents who noticed smoke coming from a house as they returned from a date may have saved the life of the woman's father, fire officials said Wednesday.

The fire apparently was started by a cigarette left burning in an ashtray, said Capt. Anne Gonzalez, city fire marshal. The owner of the house, Albert Stone of 2935 Parkway Drive, was home alone at the time.

Stone was treated for smoke inhalation at Baptist Hospital and admitted for observation. He is reported in stable condition.

Rowena Stone, the victim's daughter, and her date, Tim Stookey, 21, of 309 Lake Lane, were returning to the Stones' house and noticed the smoke. Ms. Stone and Stookey entered the house and were able to carry Stone from the burning house.

The fire was reported at 3:11 a.m. Wednesday after Ms. Stone awakened her next-door neighbor, John Perkins of 2932 Parkway Drive. The fire was under control at 4:23 a.m.

Gonzalez said there were signs that a cigarette had been left burning in the living room. "The cigarette could have fallen from an ashtray and ignited the nearby curtains," Gonzalez said.

Stone and his daughter are the only residents of the house.

The home, insured by Dominic Prado of Property and Casualty Co., Inc., is valued at $75,000. Prado said the home is insured for $79,000 and the contents for $30,000.

14. A. Obvious sources:
     a. Valentine Schettler, an Amish resident of rural Audrain County
     b. Jon Miller, another in the Amish community
     Other possible sources:
     a. University experts on Amish communities
     b. Police and sheriff's department officials on accidents involving Amish carriages
     c. Amish community residents in Ohio
     d. Religious experts
     The story is a superficial, two-source story. It is intended as a localization of a tragedy that occurred in another state. But the reporter did no more than read wire accounts of the tragedy and ask for the reaction of two local Amish residents. Much more could have been done to put the story into perspective. The preceding suggestions for additional sources show what could have been done.
   B. Obvious sources:
     a. Lynn Woolkamp, Lincoln County Sheriff's Department
     b. Statistics from the state Division of Health Resources
     c. Don Needham, director of the state Division of Highway Safety
     d. The Highway Patrol
     e. National Highway Traffic Safety Administration statistics
     f. Mothers Against Drunk Driving survey
     Other possible sources:
     a. A representative of Mothers Against Drunk Driving
     b. The parents of a teenager killed on the highways
     In general, the reporter did a good job of finding various sources to prepare this account. A couple more, as suggested here, would have helped. This story, though, is much better-reported than the previous one because it relies on more sources.

Solutions to Workbook Questions and Exercises: Court Stories Reporting

15. A. The lead to this story isn't the strongest, but the story is a compelling one. With a stronger lead, it could have been outstanding. The story is such a dramatic one that it almost writes itself. When the news is compelling, the best thing a reporter can do is let the story tell itself. In general, this writer did just that.
    B. This is a reasonably well-written update of the status of cameras in the courtroom. The writer does a good job of sprinkling quotes throughout the story. The article's main failing is its length; for the subject, the story is overwritten.
16. Here is one way to write the story:

John R. Wallinger, 29, of 202 Park Place, pleaded not guilty (Tuesday) to a charge of robbing the Black Derby Liquor Store (date).

Wallinger said he could not afford an attorney, so Magistrate Darla Mickelson appointed Public Defender Linda Treator to defend him.

Wallinger is charged with robbing the Black Derby Liquor Store, 2311 Ripley Way, of $2,845. The robber demanded cash from clerk Seve Bellinos, who triggered a silent alarm during the holdup. Police arrived in time to see the robber flee. One fired a shot at the robber, but he escaped.

More details of the robbery could be included. What really is needed is more information about the court appearance, including the bail amount set by the judge. It also would be good if the reporter could learn how police connected Wallinger to the robbery.

17. There is much information here that should not be used or should be used only after additional verification. Some of the information serves to convict the suspect in the press. Here is one way to write the story:

> Police arrested a man (Monday) who they believe may be responsible for as many as 40 burglaries during the past year.
>
> John A. Intaglio, 22, of 2909 Richardson St., was charged with the burglaries of seven northside homes and businesses. Prosecutor Ralph Gingrich said he also was charged with seven counts of stealing and four counts of selling stolen merchandise.
>
> Police Chief Antonio Grasso said investigators started checking on Intaglio after receiving reports of stolen merchandise being sold to a fence. Police have obtained a warrant for the arrest of the fence, who has left town.
>
> Grasso said some stolen merchandise was recovered from Intaglio's home.
>
> The seven burglaries with which Intaglio has been charged are:
>
> - Roger's Liquors, 202 Delmore St., $250, Sept. 8.
> - Bill Rhone Texaco, 1212 Fifth St., $23 and a calculator, Sept. 17.
> - Linda Poole's home, 2000 Dickerson Ave., $200 in cash and $300 in jewelry, Sept. 20.
> - Ron Doyle's home, 2180 Dickerson Ave., $2,000 fur coat, Sept. 26.
> - Denny Doyle's home, 209 Drolling Place, $10, Nov. 12.
> - Miller Bros. department store, 209 Main St., $2,800 in merchandise, Feb. 18.
> - Don and Linda Hopson's home, 333 E. Briarwood St., $20 and coins valued at $2,900, July 19.

18. Here is one way to write this court story:

> The attorney for a man accused of a series of northside burglaries charged (Monday) that Circuit Judge Thompson Dickerson III is prejudiced against his Italian client.
>
> Attorney Richard Delano, 2020 First St., asked for a mistrial on grounds that Dickerson dislikes Italians. He said Dickerson had tried 14 cases involving Italian defendants in the six years he has been on the bench, and all 14 had been convicted.
>
> Dickerson denied the motion and warned Delano "to concentrate on defending your client. Leave the rest to me. I can assure you that I like Italians, and I like pizza, too."
>
> Delano is a well-known criminal lawyer who handled the murder case of John D'Aquisto, who was found innocent of murdering First Ward Councilman Roger Baker last year.

The seven burglaries with which Intaglio has been charged are:

- Roger's Liquors, 202 Delmore St., $250, Sept. 8.
- Bill Rhone Texaco, 1212 Fifth St., $23 and a calculator, Sept. 17.
- Linda Poole's home, 2000 Dickerson Ave., $200 in cash and $300 in jewelry, Sept. 20.
- Ron Doyle's home, 2180 Dickerson Ave., $2,000 fur coat, Sept. 26.
- Denny Doyle's home, 209 Drolling Place, $10, Nov. 12.
- Miller Bros. department store, 209 Main St., $2,800 in merchandise, Feb. 18.
- Don and Linda Hopson's home, 333 E. Briarwood St., $20 and coins valued at $2,900, July 19.

During Monday's testimony, Police Detective William O'Shaunessy testified that stolen merchandise found in Intaglio's home was positively identified by the owners.

When O'Shaunessy volunteered that Intaglio had admitted to police that he had stolen the items, Delano objected and asked for a mistrial. The judge denied that motion but ruled the testimony inadmissible and instructed the jury to ignore it.

19. Here is one way to write the acquittal story:

John A. Intaglio was acquitted (Tuesday) of burglarizing seven homes and businesses in the northside area.

The jury deliberated only 20 minutes before returning its verdict. None of the jurors would comment on the decision.

"I'm appalled," said Prosecutor Ralph Gingrich. "I thought our case was airtight. We'll have another chance, though. We plan to try him in connection with some other burglaries."

Defense attorney Richard Delano said his client was innocent and a victim of persecution by the police, the prosecutor and the judge. "A wise jury saw through all that," he said.

The seven burglaries with which Intaglio had been charged are:

- Roger's Liquors, 202 Delmore St., $250, Sept. 8.
- Bill Rhone Texaco, 1212 Fifth St., $23 and a calculator, Sept. 17.
- Linda Poole's home, 2000 Dickerson Ave., $200 in cash and $300 in jewelry, Sept. 20.
- Ron Doyle's home, 2180 Dickerson Ave., $2,000 fur coat, Sept. 26.
- Denny Doyle's home, 209 Drolling Place, $10, Nov. 12.
- Miller Bros. department store, 209 Main St., $2,800 in merchandise, Feb. 18.
- Don and Linda Hopson's home, 333 E. Briarwood St., $20 and coins valued at $2,900, July 19.

20. a. *Misdemeanor:* A crime classified as a minor offense. Some crimes may be misdemeanors in one state and felonies in another.
    b. *Felony:* A crime classified as serious, including murder, rape and grand theft.
    c. *Preliminary hearing:* A hearing to determine if there is probable cause to hold a defendant for further court action in a higher court.

d. *Arraignment:* The procedure in which a judge informs the defendant of the charge against him or her and advises the defendant of the right to counsel. Often the defendant is asked to enter a plea.

e. *Probable cause:* A determination by a judge that there is sufficient reason to believe a crime has been committed and that the defendant committed it.

f. *Grand jury:* A citizen panel charged with reviewing evidence in secret to determine whether an indictment—or charge—should be issued.

g. *True bill:* An indictment.

h. *Not true bill:* A refusal to indict.

i. *Indictment:* A grand jury charge that an individual or group has committed a crime.

j. *Information:* A charge filed by a prosecutor in some states as an alternative to indictment.

k. *Plea bargaining:* The procedure in which a defendant pleads guilty to a lesser charge. This saves the state the expense of a trial and allows the defendant to avoid the possibility of conviction for a more serious offense.

l. *Change of venue:* A change in the location of a trial or other court proceeding.

21. Because the prosecutor must show that a crime was committed and that there is reason to believe that the defendant committed it, a preliminary hearing may reveal much about what happened and the nature of evidence against the accused.

22. The two attorneys are the most likely sources. The judge cannot talk about the case for obvious reasons, and restrictions about discussing the case will have been placed on the police. Although the attorneys may be under similar restraints—either self-imposed or imposed by the judge— they are likely to be the only potential sources for comment.

23. If you want to understand the court system, it helps to view it firsthand. That is the purpose of this exercise, which can be done with any court. Traffic cases are suggested here merely because they are usually easy to understand. More complicated cases may baffle the courtroom newcomer.

24. This exercise is an extension of exercise 23. Here, however, the student should be able to obtain information about the crime from morgue files. Your ability to assign this exercise will depend on the level of activity at the local courthouse. In some rural areas, it may be impractical.

25. Obvious sources:
    a. Rahsetnu Miller, associate public defender
    b. Court records
    Other possible sources:
    a. Prosecutors
    b. Local police
    c. Mississippi authorities

26. Key figures in the O.J. Simpson case:
    a. O.J. Simpson, the accused
    b. Marcia Clark, the prosecutor
    c. Lance Ito, the judge
    d. Johnnie Cochran, defense attorney

    e. Robert Shapiro, defense attorney
    f. F. Lee Bailey, defense attorney
    g. Numerous witnesses

27. **CHALLENGE EXERCISE.** There are many similarities between the Sheppard case and the Simpson case. But today's instantaneous television coverage makes the Simpson case even more of a problem. In the Simpson case, the jury was sequestered throughout. That was not done in the Sheppard case, a critical factor in his acquittal.

PART FIVE: BEAT REPORTING

CHAPTER 14: COVERING A BEAT

Overview

As you know, the only way to really learn how to cover a beat is to cover one. Your students probably will have to seek that opportunity outside this course, on the student newspaper or in advanced courses. This chapter is intended to prepare them.

In some programs, this chapter and those that follow are used in a course in which actual beat reporting is possible. That is a good option. If it's not the option you choose, you can still achieve realism with the exercises in the textbook and the workbook. You may want to add to that realism by arranging guest lectures by professionals who cover beats at your local newspaper or station.

The procedures that seem most difficult for beginning reporters are developing sources and learning to think in terms of readers' or viewers' interests. You may want to emphasize these steps.

And, as always, you are welcome to supplement the exercises, examples and anecdotes included here with your own.

Solutions to Textbook Questions and Exercises

1. Since this exercise is designed to introduce students to the real world of beat reporting, you'll want to make sure that both sources and story ideas are applicable to actual local circumstances.
2. Chapter 5, Gathering Information, provides the help students will need with background. The second part of the exercise requires local homework.
3. Students will have an array of newspapers from which to choose. Now that a growing number of papers are putting their work into cyberspace, the array is even greater.

    The differences between those papers that see themselves as national, such as *The New York Times*, *The Wall Street Journal* and *USA Today*, and those that maintain a local focus should show up both in story topics and in how those stories are written. The same congressional story, for instance, is likely to be told differently in *USA Today* and in the *Detroit Free Press*, which will look for the story's impact on its own region and its own readers.

    Students are also likely to notice greater reliance in Washington on official sources, often unnamed, and less reaction or comment from unofficial "real people."
4. Answers will vary. Compare the sources suggested in the textbook to the sources students use.

Solutions to Workbook Questions and Exercises

1. Some students in your class may be working on the campus paper. If so, they can supply firsthand knowledge. Interviewing them or inviting into

class the student editor can supplement the kind of content analysis this exercise requires.

Students probably will find a lot of mimicking of professional approaches. Many student papers, like their commercial counterparts, are overly reliant on official sources and press releases. A good measure of the quality of the student paper is the extent to which its coverage seems to be reader-driven and not source-driven. Another good measure is the extent to which reporters seek out nonofficial (student or faculty) comment and perspective.

2. The most obvious sources on the central administration beat are, of course, the administrators themselves. That's fine. The more imaginative students—and those who take seriously the urgings of this chapter—will include secretaries and low-level functionaries. Student consumers should show up on everybody's lists.

   The techniques for earning confidence are detailed in the chapter. Demonstrating background knowledge and ensuring accuracy are the most important.

   For a first story, students should be sure to pick an issue or a personality with high interest among prospective readers. The rationale for the choice is more important than the topic itself.

3. The point here is to introduce the student reporter to local government by putting principles into practice. Ask for sources of information in the memo to be sure important bases are covered. Demand specifics. Students' reasons for choosing their sources are more important than the sources themselves. The local newspaper will provide lots of clues.

4. The same principles apply as in exercise 3.

5. The most likely sources should include campus experts and community or state officials responsible for enforcement of environmental protection. Scholarly and popular publications are available in university and public libraries and, increasingly, via computer. Specific choices are less important than the reasons behind the choices. The chapter itself offers some starter suggestions.

6. a. Students should ask the readers' questions outlined in the chapter. There are many unanswered questions about costs and benefits, including the possibility of a conflict of interest on Mayor Williams' part. Be sure students would talk to opponents.

   b. The answer comes straight from the section that follows in the chapter.

7-9. The stories will vary from city to city. However, issues such as religion and politics, medical and scientific ethics, or the costs of environmental cleanups can be found anywhere. Resources should include documentary sources for background (suggestions can be found in Chapters 2 and 5 in addition to this chapter) and local human sources, who can be found (or at least their offices located) in references such as the campus directory, the city telephone book and the local paper. You'll want to make sure that the stories you assign can be completed within students' limits of time and resources.

10. **CHALLENGE EXERCISE.** The point of this exercise should be obvious to students. By explaining issues in advance, and by including information on the next step in the decision-making process, reporters can empower readers to be participants rather than mere onlookers as important

issues are debated. The combination of stories gives students practice in researching issues, requires them to look for sources beyond the official ones, and then provides the experience of covering a public meeting.

Students should have no trouble finding other examples in either campus or community newspapers. Emphasize to them the importance of including the "empowerment" information that tells readers how they can get involved.

CHAPTER 15: BUSINESS AND CONSUMER NEWS

Overview

Students' enthusiasm for business journalism is rising, as is the number of jobs in the field. It is important for you to encourage students to think as business journalists. As we have noted in the chapter, everything that isn't handled by government is provided by business. And many government decisions spawn business stories.

This chapter introduces some basic business and economic terms, which we have tried to translate. You may want to supplement this information by having students read *The Wall Street Journal*, *Kiplinger's Personal Finance*, *Money* magazine, *Forbes*, *Fortune* or one of the dozens of other business-related publications. Point out to them that these are also potential well-paying employers.

Beginning journalists often have a negative attitude toward the profit motive, so it is important for you to stress balance. Students need to remember that without profit, businesses couldn't pay wages, people wouldn't have jobs and the economy would fall apart.

Consumer pieces written by beginning journalists are often blatantly biased against the company. Watch for this, and teach students how to write an objective piece.

There are many eye-opening ways to make young students aware of and more comfortable with business issues. Having them invest imaginary money through an online service or a stock market game introduces them to the world of investment. Taking them to a local bank and having a loan officer walk them through the costs of a home mortgage often gets their attention. You can also invite CEOs for the area's dominant industries in to speak. Hospital CEOs can talk about health care as a business; real estate agents can talk about housing and construction; manufacturers can talk about employment rates and their impact on hiring and wages.

Periodic math quizzes with questions like those included in the workbook can ease students' minds about math. Field trips to the assessor's office, the business license office or a local company can add color and insight to the class. You could also ask students to analyze stories throughout the paper and explain how some of them could be turned into business pieces.

Solutions to Textbook Questions and Exercises

1. Given the premise that any story can be a business story, it does not take much imagination for students to transform front-page news into business news. A story about the use of a bond issue to construct a new

school, for example, can turn into an analysis of how much money such a project could generate in the local economy, depending on whether a local or out-of-town builder is used. It can discuss the types of businesses likely to open on surrounding parcels of land, or potential changes in home building patterns in the area.

A story about the new football coach at the local college can inspire stories on how the team's record affects the local economy, with a special emphasis on restaurants, hotels and souvenir shops.

A story on pesticides in a local stream can lead to a feature on an environmental cleanup company, an analysis of the availability of waste disposal facilities in the area, or an investigation of the impact of rumored pollution on tourism.

Encourage students to search for the unusual story, not the easy or obvious one.

2. Some students are naturally competitive and will get a charge out of comparing their portfolio's progress with that of their classmates. Others need the added incentive of a weekly report that requires them to analyze how issues in the news affected their stock. If a major sports figure signs on as a spokesperson for a shoe company, for example, it is easy to see what happens to the price of the stock. Less-publicized events, however, will have an impact. If a company is accused of violating antitrust laws, cited by the Environmental Protection Agency for violating pollution codes, or boycotted by a consumer group for animal rights offenses, students will see the stock drop. It helps to have them write a weekly report that explains any movement in their stocks.

3. A stockbroker or financial adviser can help students understand the different investment strategies people use, depending on whether they're investing for a time well into the future and therefore willing to take some risks, or looking for conservative, steady paybacks in the near future. Once they understand these differences, students are better able to detect the target audience for the prospectus.

Either prospectus will give students more information on a company than they knew existed. Comparing several within the same industry will be particularly educational.

4. Use the 10-K report to analyze whether this company is one students would like to invest in or if they can find a story buried in the numbers that might be of interest to local readers. If there is a story there, have them write it up as if it were going into the local paper.

Solutions to Workbook Questions and Exercises

1. a. The lead should be fairly close to this one:

   > Universal Conglomerate Co. announced today that it plans to merge with International Conglomerate Co., becoming the largest company in the United States.

   b. Questions: Why is the merger taking place? What does the government say? What about areas in which the two companies now compete? What are the terms of the merger? What happens to the stock?

2. A possible approach:

> The chairman of Universal Motors Corp. complained today that car prices have been forced up $1,000 by safety equipment urged by consumer groups and required by the government.
>
> A consumer group spokesperson replied that Universal Motors Chairman J.B. Grebe "should be declared a public criminal" for opposing mandatory safety features.
>
> And a federal safety official agreed with Grebe's figures but insisted that the required equipment is saving 10,000 lives a year. . . .

3. The necessary directories are discussed in the chapter and should be available in the college or public library. These can also be found online in corporate profiles.
4. Reading the newspaper and using the telephone book are probably the only steps needed. You can require students to justify their choices.
5. The necessary directories and sources are discussed in the chapter and should be available in the college or public library.
6. Read the annual report, 10-K and proxy as indicated in the text. This should prepare you for explaining the key points noted in the question.
7. You will need to analyze at least some of the same stories because the bias of students as well as that of the stories is being tested. Question every conclusion you can, so as to make students think through their answers.
8. This is the basic consumer story. After students complete the assignment, you may want to discuss why so few newspapers do that kind of story. The possible loss of grocery ads, the life's blood of many small- and medium-sized papers, is the most obvious inhibitor, of course.
9. This exercise should help encourage students to examine what impact news stories have on the market.
10. Online corporate profiles analyze the history and potential of companies. They also list officers, income, expenses and stock prices. Students should be able to see who has been a market leader in the past and who might become one in the future.
11. a. As a percentage, their raise will be 15.75 percent. In dollars, it would be $3,938. It would not be different if it were given in a different order. To find this number, multiply $25,000 by 1.06 to get 26,500. Multiply 26,500 by 1.04 to get 27,560. Multiply 27,560 by 1.05 to get 28,938, which would be the salary after the three raises.
   b. They were being paid $24,175.82. To find this number, divide 22,000 by 0.91. (The 0.91 represents the percentage of the teachers' original salary that is left after a pay cut of 0.09, or 9 percent.)
   c. The answer is 50 percent. (It's a trick question—6 minus 4 is 2, and 2 is 50 percent of 4.)
   d. $190,000. To find this number, divide 127,300 by 0.67.
   e. The company's weekly payroll is $136,621.87; its annual payroll is $7,104,337.20 ($7.1 million).
      The *multiplier effect* is a term used by economists to explain the idea that people cash their paychecks and then spend money throughout the community. That money then becomes wages and profits, which are also spent throughout the community. The multiplier effect varies

depending on whether most of a community's wages stay within the community or are spent elsewhere—in a nearby city, for example. In this case, the economic impact of the plant's closing would be $21.3 million, or $21,313,011.

f. $126.50. To find this number divide 3 by 8 to get 0.375. Subtract 37.5 cents from your $32 per share price to get $31.625 per share. Multiply this by the 400 shares you own to get $126.50.

g. The salaries would be $154 apart the first year, $250 the second, and $329 the third. The school district would save $42,350 the first year, $68,750 the second, and $90,475 the third. Over the three years, it would save $201,575. To find these numbers, use the same math as in problem 11.a.

h. *Red-light* numbers are those that are incredibly unlikely because of some pre-existing limit, such as the population of the town, state or country. If a local pizza outlet claims it will sell 100,000 pizzas this weekend, but your town only has a population of 50,000, you should be skeptical. In this case, the population of the whole nation is about 280 million, so the computer company would have to sell a computer to nearly every other person in the United States.

12. **CHALLENGE EXERCISE.**
a. The money left over after all income and costs, including extraordinary ones, are considered.

b. Net income divided by the number of shares outstanding.

c. Obviously, if the net income is divided among fewer shares, the earnings per share will be higher.

d. A possible lead: Gannett, the company that publishes *USA Today*, saw its net income jump 10 percent in the first three months of this year. The company made a profit of $86.2 million, compared with $78.7 million at the same time last year.

e. The Gannett company has subsidiaries throughout the United States. Perhaps the company has billboards in your community. Or maybe the local paper has trouble competing with *USA Today*. Gannett also gives money to various educational institutions and charities, some of which might be in your town.

CHAPTER 16: SPORTS

Overview

The theme of this chapter is that the quality of sports reporting can be and should be as high as the quality of any other reporting. Too often it isn't. Too often sportswriters forget that they must be reporters, or journalists, first and always. So the emphasis in this chapter, in its principles and examples, is on the application to sports of the techniques of any good reporting and writing.

You'll probably have in your class some students who are sports fans and who would like nothing better than to write, even to live, sports. For them, the limitations of their knowledge as fans and the requirements of solid reporting will be the real lessons. Other students will know and care nothing about sports. For them, this chapter can be a broadening experience, perhaps demonstrating the opportunities sport offers for exploring the human condition.

For all students, and for you, this chapter should also be fun. It may offer an opportunity for some creativity and lightheartedness that can get lost in the serious business of journalism. Make sure you send your students out to the games—any games.

Solutions to Textbook Questions and Exercises

1. The sources are discussed in the chapter, as are possible story ideas. You'll need to make sure that both lists are realistic in relation to local circumstances.
2. The comparison will be the interesting part. Unless you are at the University of Texas or one of a very few other schools where women's sports have achieved some approximation of parity, your students will find great disparities, despite federal regulations, in everything from facilities to fan support. These disparities, of course, should suggest stories.
3. The definition of a "minor" sport varies, of course. The point of the exercise is to broaden students' horizons beyond the often overcovered "major" sports.
4. This, of course, is the way sports reporters or any others really begin to learn their craft.
5. Some of the best sports writing anywhere appears in *Sports Illustrated*, so it won't be surprising if the magazine comes out ahead. And, unlike many magazine comparisons, time alone often isn't an adequate explanation for the differences. Sharp-eyed reporting and a fine touch with the language are the keys.
6. Cyberspace is full of conversations about sports, fantasy sports leagues of all sorts, and more statistics and background material than anyone can digest. Indeed, there's so much available that another question might be: What does all this tell you about the competition faced by reporters covering sports for traditional media? And the answer to that is that the competition is so fierce that the level of reporting and storytelling must rise if audiences are to be kept satisfied.

Solutions to Workbook Questions and Exercises

1. For the fans among your students, this will be a delight. For the others, it will be a chore, but an educational one. They'll find sports everywhere—on local broadcast channels, on specialty channels, on superchannels, even on CNN.
2. Now comes the hard part—competing. Fortunately, a large part of the answer is easy. ESPN doesn't cover high school sports or the kids' soccer league. Local papers or stations can and must. Nor are you likely to find much real storytelling on the tube. That's what the newspaper can do. You can also get behind the scenes and beyond the glare of the spotlights to cover the nonstars and the nonrevenue sports. Those are also the sports that most people are likely to play.
3. Television has the great advantage of the moving picture. That's great for reporting on contests. Television, when it is done well, can also capture

the drama of an individual athlete in victory or failure. Television, in other words, can *show*. So that's what students should plan to do. Depth and detail, on the other hand, are the natural province of print.

4. As the truly mass medium, television sports is likely to focus on the events with mass appeal—the professional contests and the college revenue sports—with feature coverage of local high school stars. If the newspaper is a good one, you'll find more depth and more breadth. Each medium is playing to its strength.

5. Your students should find a wealth of high school coverage in both media. They should note the differences pointed out before. What they're likely to find, though, is that the stories are told from the adult perspective, through the words of coaches and parents rather than the players. Some of that results from the reasonable protectiveness school officials may exercise over young athletes. Some of it, though, probably results from laziness or lack of imagination (or lack of time) on the part of reporters who take the most accessible sources. As journalists try to lure young audiences, that should be changing.

6. The answers are suggested in the chapter and in the results of the preceding exercises. Coaches, stars and boosters are obvious sources. The better the reporter, the wider the range of less obvious sources—the benchwarmers, the participants in less visible sports, parents, teachers and so on.

7. a. The average number of earned runs a pitcher allows per nine innings; it is figured by multiplying the number of earned runs by nine, then dividing the results by the number of innings pitched.

   $7 \times 9 = 63$ divided by $27 = 2.33$

   b. The number of hits divided by the number of official at bats (walks and sacrifices are not official at bats).

   57 divided by $212 = .269$

   c. Hits plus walks plus hit-by-pitch divided by at bats plus walks plus hit-by-pitch plus sacrifices.

   76 divided by $212 = .358$ (assumes no hit-by-pitches)

8-9. The same principles apply to both. These are participant sports at most schools, so the names won't be as well-known and the coverage in the local newspaper probably will be "minor" too. However, students will find stars and benchwarmers, winners and losers, caring coaches and noncaring ones in any sport. Encourage students to read specialty publications so that they can develop some expertise.

10. Of course, the definition of "participant" will vary by locality. Rodeo may not be a participant sport in Texas, nor ice hockey in Minnesota. The idea is to force students to look beyond the stadiums and the crowds.

11. Here's one acceptable lead:

Fresno Pacific outmuscled and outshot Springfield College, 81-56. Muldrow provided the only bright spot for Springfield, with 20 points and 9 rebounds.

12. The questions are obvious. The statistics provide clues to "how" and "why," but they don't provide answers. Nor do they give basics such as the backgrounds of the teams or even the first names of the players. The list of questions should be a lengthy one.
13. Notice the perspective and analysis provided by both the reporter and the coach. We learn not only that the local team lost, but how and why. This is a game story that adds to what even the most observant fan could have seen at courtside or on television.
14. The choices are many. You may want to require memos on the preparation and to assign deadlines for the stories. It will be easier for you to check on students' work if you send the whole class, or at least several members, to the same event.
15. **CHALLENGE EXERCISE.** The better the idea, the better the story. However, make sure the idea you assign can actually be completed within the time available. Some ideas aren't feasible for beginning reporters working with limited time.

PART SIX: SPECIALIZED TECHNIQUES

CHAPTER 17: SOCIAL SCIENCE REPORTING

Overview

The primary purpose of this chapter is to introduce students to a way of thinking about reporting that is more important than even many professionals realize. We also want to provide a chance for some beginning practice in techniques that will be even more important in years to come.

As you know, few practicing journalists spend much time thinking of reporting as a social science. More than a few probably would resist the very idea. However, we think—and we hope you agree—that the relationship exists and should be strengthened. This chapter assumes very little background in the vocabulary or the techniques of social science. Students who come to the chapter with more background can move to the more advanced exercises and develop their skills. For most students, however, we think a reasonable outcome is an understanding of what the social sciences have to offer to reporters.

The exercises, as always, are designed to put concepts into practice. You're a better judge than we can be of your students' ability and inclination to tackle actual surveys or experiments.

Solutions to Textbook Questions and Exercises

1. Such stories appear frequently in nearly every newspaper. The most common flaws are failures to describe methodology and to discuss margin of error.
2. This isn't as hard as it may look. The key will be deciding on the population to be surveyed and then selecting the sample. For most practical purposes, the local telephone book or student directory provides an adequate source. Meyer and others offer fairly simple methods for assuring random selection.
3. Examples of such experiments are described in the chapter. Remember that the hypothesis must be capable of being proved or disproved and the variables must be adequately controlled.
4. Have your students conduct a survey.
5. If you don't have the background to handle the data analysis, there should be colleagues willing to help. Computer programs that perform the analysis are now available even for microcomputers.

Solutions to Workbook Questions and Exercises

1. Chances are, important information will be left out. Typically, newspaper reports do include the margin of error and the sponsor of the survey. But the questions themselves are almost never reproduced. Also nearly always missing is crucial information on the size of subgroups and the error margins for those findings. Students should come away from this exercise and the one that follows with a healthy sense of caution about the reporting of surveys.

2. Broadcasters usually are even worse than print journalists at leaving out crucial information. The missing information could often be supplied easily and clearly in a graphic. What students should realize is that the cause of the missing information usually isn't technical difficulty but lack of understanding by the journalists of the information's importance. This is a key point of the chapter.

3. The omissions, as noted before, probably will be significant. A frequent result of such omissions is that the results are presented as more certain and more definitive than they really are. It would be instructive for students to interview a researcher for a firsthand account of the dangers of underreporting and overreliance.

4. Student stories are almost certain to be superior to the professional versions. This should be not only educational but morale-boosting, as the students see that they can do something better than it is usually done.

5. This story follows most of the guidelines. The explanatory paragraph is more complete than students will find in most professionally written stories. Even here, though, we're not given the actual questions. Nor are we told the number of nonresponses, which should be taken as a measure of real public awareness or concern.

   The most important problem with this story, however, is typical of survey reporting. It doesn't allow for any expression of subtle distinctions or complexity. For instance, what do people really mean by "crime"? Are they actually afraid of being assaulted in the streets, or are they expressing more complicated concerns? This is a limitation of the methodology itself—one that few journalists seem to understand.

   Still, even with its limitations, this kind of bottom-up reporting can make a real contribution to a campaign by showing what's really on the minds of the electorate, instead of just allowing the candidates to set the agenda.

6. Keeping in mind the limitations just mentioned, a survey-literate editor might assign more in-depth reporting to explore those complexities and connections. An even more obvious follow-up is to question the candidates about their plans to respond to constituent concerns.

7. As the chapter points out, person-on-the-street interviews really have limited, if any, value. Scientific surveying, despite its limitations, has the great virtue of sampling the opinions and ideas of a cross-section of the community instead of relying solely on the voices of self-selected activists and the candidates themselves. Surveys, supplemented by in-depth interviewing, can contribute to the democratic process by bringing the real issues to the surface and by requiring candidates to respond. And this is a service only journalists are likely to perform.

8. Depending on the relationship between newspaper and station, you might want to report on the survey itself. You might want to commission your own studies. You might want to point out the limitations of the newspaper survey. You might even sponsor a public gathering, which you'd then cover, to foster public discussion of the issues.

9. a. Handling the problem of invasion of privacy: As with the other two types of problems with this project, there is no real "answer." The important point is sensitivity to the privacy rights and the human feelings of those being observed. However, the purpose of such a project

will be defeated if the reporter does not look closely and record the details he or she observes. As in reporting of almost any kind, what is required is a kind of balancing act between the legitimate interests of the public and the legitimate rights of individuals.

b. The problem of involvement: The same lack of firm rules operates here. The chapter outlines the most likely traps; students should demonstrate awareness of them—the best protection against getting caught in one.

c. The problem of generalizing: This is simpler than the other two problem areas. Avoidance requires no more than the self-discipline that should be part of any reporting assignment—going no further in the story than the information available will allow.

10. Once you've made sure that the proposed projects are at least theoretically feasible, we suggest relying on the *Handbook of Reporting Methods* and *The Reporters' Handbook* (see the Suggested Readings for Chapter 18, Investigative Reporting) for specific tips on how to proceed and where to look for the records. Good projects don't have to be complicated ones.

11. The example of the male and female loan applicants is a good one to follow. The hypothesis must be capable of being proved or disproved. Another key is the controlling of as many variables as possible.

12. a. *Random sample:* A group chosen so that every member of the population has an equal chance of being selected.

b. *Chi square:* A statistical test of the significance of results.

c. *Mean:* The average of a group of numbers arrived at by adding all the numbers and dividing by the number of figures in the group.

d. *Median:* The midpoint in a list of numbers arranged in order of size. Half the numbers are below the median and half are above it.

e. *Mode:* The most frequent number in a group.

f. *Stratified sample:* One picked so as to ensure that each subgroup in the population is represented.

g. *Validity:* The degree to which an experiment measures what it purports to measure.

h. *Reliability:* The extent to which an experiment could be repeated with the same results.

13. Almost certainly, the analyses will turn up significant failures to apply the guidelines. The consequences of such failures can be serious, for both journalists and readers.

14. You'll want to keep this as simple as possible. As long as students understand the problems involved in doing so, use the telephone book or student directory to draw a sample. You probably have access to a computer with the SPSS software, which will perform all the statistical tests and cross-tabulations that students will need. One of the most useful resource books is Meyer's *Precision Journalism*.

15. **CHALLENGE EXERCISE.**

a. Suggestion: a pie chart.

b. How were the subjects selected? What are the demographics (sex, family income, education levels of parents, location)? What questions were asked and what was the exact wording?

c. Nonrandom selection of subjects, skewed demographics (toward males or well-to-do families, for example), leading wording of questions.

d. Probable focus of lead: children's view that there is too much sex on television.

16. **CHALLENGE EXERCISE.** This exercise should impress on students both the possibilities and the difficulties of scientific reporting. Keeping in mind that students will need to get people into the story, have students solicit comments to supplement the statistics and seek permission to use names with the best comments. Rely on Meyer's book for guidance. You may want to do some checking of your own to be sure that no student filled out his or her own questionnaire.

CHAPTER 18: INVESTIGATIVE REPORTING

Overview

This chapter, like others, has been reworked to emphasize the growing importance of the computer as an essential tool for serious reporting. However, the foundation of the chapter remains its discussion of sources and techniques, traditional as well as computer-based.

Most introductory books don't include a chapter on investigative reporting. We do, for two reasons. First, investigative journalism is such an important part of the field (and seems likely to grow even further in importance) that we think any practitioner or consumer of journalism should have some understanding of its purposes and techniques. Second, those students who intend to become reporters will find this chapter a solid foundation for more advanced work.

One chapter, of course, does not an investigative reporter make. We think this chapter can introduce attitudes and skills that can be applied to any reporting assignment. We also think it important that beginners start with an appreciation of the importance and the limitations of this highest form of reporting.

The exercises are intended to include both some that are within the reach of almost any student and a few that will stretch your best students.

Solutions to Textbook Questions and Exercises

1. a. The sniff: A good place to start is with the complaining school board member. What does she know and how does she know it? Are there other critics of the architect or superintendent who might be helpful? What do public records show about the superintendent's land ownership, taxes paid, business partnerships and so on?
   b. Human sources: See a.; also consider other architects who might resent unfair competition, other school system officials and any enemies of the superintendent or architect. Start with the outspoken critic; save the architect and superintendent for last.
   c. Records: The chapter describes the most likely ones. *The Reporters' Handbook* (see Suggested Readings) will help.
   d. The most you can prove is that the suspected payoffs actually occurred. You'll still have a good story if you demonstrate incompetence or favoritism short of corruption.

2. The public records are those identified in the chapter, plus any others you may be aware of in your area. You'll want to make sure that students have looked at the obvious ones, including the following:

- Property ownership and tax records
- Vehicle registration and driver's license data
- Voter registration information
- Any available records on mortgages or other borrowings
- Legal records, such as lawsuits, divorces and so on

3. Valuable as they are, computer databases seldom include the details and anecdotes you need to make a member of Congress or anyone else come alive in a story. You're likely to find biographical and political data, voting record, campaign contributions, even travel spending and honorariums. You'll still need interviews to supply the human element.

Solutions to Workbook Questions and Exercises

1. Use a broad enough definition of investigative reporting to include both the relatively few megaprojects you'll find and the more frequent examinations of problems and abuses that get at least somewhat below the surface of events. You'll probably find a mix of those stories that focus on individual problems (probably the majority of the stories) and the more sophisticated examinations of systems.

2. As you know, the success of CBS's *60 Minutes* spawned a school of imitators on the major networks, to say nothing of the pseudojournalism of programs such as *Inside Edition* and *Hard Copy*. Though the number of programs fluctuates, there's a lot of investigative reporting—of a sort—on network television. Typically, your students will find less investigative reporting at the local level, though that will vary from market to market.

   As you'd expect, newspapers are stronger on detail and documentation. Television, as always, relies more on visual storytelling. Television reporters ask viewers to accept without attribution more of what they say. Students should weigh the benefits of storytelling against the cost in depth. Print-oriented students especially may want to consider whether television has lessons to teach newspapers when it comes to conveying complex issues understandably.

3. Most local news organizations don't do as much investigating as they should. Many probably do as much as they can, given limitations of staff and budget. At its best, as in Minneapolis, Miami or Akron, local investigative reporting can match anything you're likely to see in the national media. At its worst, the local variety can be not really investigative at all.

4. Most of this information can be found in places other than the Internet, of course, but requiring students to use the Internet will make them more comfortable with it, and they will discover the range of data available quickly and easily. One caution: Internet addresses do change.
   a. U.S. Department of Commerce, Bureau of Census:
      http://www.census.gov
   b. U.S. Department of Commerce, STAT-USA:
      http://www.stat-usa.gov/stat-usa.html

c. You can find the most recent crime report from the U.S. Department of Justice, Bureau of Justice Statistics:
   http://www.ojp.usdoj.gov/bjs/pubalp2.html

d. Computer sales are compiled by the U.S. Department of Commerce, Office of Computers and Business Equipment:
   http://infoserv2.ita.doc.gov/ocbe/ocbehome.nsf

5. Here's an outline of a possible memo:

   The topic: Allegations of sexual harassment in the student services office. Why: It's illegal. It's especially important on a campus where the majority of students are female. The administration doesn't seem to be doing anything.

   The sniff: Quietly interview female staff members and students who frequent the office of the associate dean we suspect. I'll track down a couple of former employees who have less to fear if they talk.

   Human sources: See previous. I'll also talk to the campus official responsible for investigating such complaints. I'll check with the associate dean's colleagues at his former college. I'll talk to higher-ups in the administration and, of course, the suspect himself.

   Documents: University records are closed, so I'll have to see if any disgruntled staffer will give me a peek. I'll check with the state and federal offices of the Equal Opportunity Commission to see if complaints have been filed. I'll also check for lawsuits.

   Computer: Most of these records are stored on computer, but I can't get access by myself. I'll do a database search and call IRE to see who else has done similar investigations and what I can learn from those.

6. The format can follow the outline in exercise 5. What you're looking for is the student's thinking process, evidence of background research and realism in the estimates of time and story likelihood.

7. The investigation described in the memo was too complex and time-consuming to be within the reach of even the most advanced student. It arose from good beat reporting. It overcame obstacles that included delay and outright lies. It resulted in a state investigation and pledges of reform. The follow-ups continued for more than a year. The real purpose of this exercise is to give students an inside look at a major investigation from the reporter's perspective.

8. a. *The sniff:* First, you need names and possible connections. The state corporations division (probably in the secretary of state's or attorney general's office) will have names of the trucking corporation's officers and major stockholders. The Interstate Commerce Commission and the Labor Department will have useful records too. And look for Maxwell's enemies in the union, as well as people who have run afoul of the trucking company. See the chapter for suggestions.

   b. *Human sources:* Several obvious ones are named in 9.a. Try to tap law enforcement officials and would-be reformers, within either the union or the company. Former members or employees may be helpful.

   c. *Records:* Both state and federal regulators watch over unions and corporations. Some are mentioned in 9.a. See *The Reporters' Handbook* for other suggestions.

96

d. The most you can hope to prove is the connection, which would be illegal. Any other connections, even if less formal, could be interesting and important.

9. What you see here is just the opening chapter in one of the most ambitious local investigative projects in recent years. In fact, this project went beyond traditional investigative reporting into an attempt to offer solutions to the problems identified by the reporting. So it is both an investigative effort and an example of "public journalism."

   The reporting techniques, as Bob Paynter explains in the chapter, ranged from old-fashioned street reporting to computer analysis of census and other data.

   The complexity and sensitivity of the topic would deter many news organizations. Akron's effort, in its full scope, is unprecedented as far as we know.

10. The planning process is the same as in exercise 8. The major differences will be in sources. Chapters 8 and 11 of *The Reporters' Handbook* will be especially helpful.

11. You are looking here for both a recognition of the problems discussed in the chapter and some imagination in suggesting ways to solve them. Possibilities: The reporter could use some of his or her own time, bring another reporter into the project to trade off on routine coverage, or bite off only a small chunk of the overall story at one time.

12. **CHALLENGE EXERCISE.**
    a. This covers ground similar to that in exercises 8 and 10.
    b. Points that should be included in the responses are covered in the chapter. Be critical of simplistic or unrealistic proposals. For example, if a student says she would quit, ask what she would do then. Wouldn't it be better to stay to fight another day? Try to emphasize that there are no easy answers.

PART SEVEN: WRITING FOR SPECIFIC MEDIA

CHAPTER 19: WRITING NEWS FOR RADIO AND TELEVISION

Overview

Although the primary purpose of this book is to prepare students to write for newspapers, much of what is discussed applies equally to writing broadcast news. In many schools of journalism, all would-be reporters begin in the same newswriting course. Further, broadcast newswriters no longer have to work on newspapers before entering their field.

Even though most of your students may not be headed toward broadcast newswriting, you may still want them to read this chapter and complete the exercises. After all, they may someday make the switch, and at the very least they will have been exposed to the differences between writing for newspaper and for broadcast news.

This chapter summarizes the differences in selecting, writing and preparing the copy for newspaper and news broadcasting. For the interested student or for the one who wants to go further into writing for broadcast, we recommend Ted White's *Broadcast News Writing and Reporting,* Second Edition (New York: St. Martin's, 1996).

We discuss writing lead-ins and writing for videotape because this chapter would be incomplete without mentioning these important parts of broadcast writing. However, the discussion is brief, and we see no practical way to give students exercises. These skills must be practiced in a course in broadcast writing.

In the section on preparing copy, you must stress that different styles are used by different stations. For example, some stations still capitalize all the copy that is to be read. However, we believe the suggestions in this chapter are practical, logical and consistent.

Solutions to Textbook Questions and Exercises

1. We recommend that you assign the class a particular newscast and a particular newspaper. You'll have a lively class discussion with the results.
2. The purpose here is analysis and discussion. Although these stories are from the broadcast wire service, they are not written in the best broadcast style. Some broadcasters would say that's because sometimes they are written by print journalists. Let's look at them briefly:
   a. The lead-in is catchy, and the verb "is bringing" is in the present progressive. The sentences are all simple sentences. Note the passive voice in "is seen." "Recently" is always a weak, meaningless adverb.
   b. Note the good use of the dashes in the story. Note also the present tense and the contractions (he's, she's). Good copy.
   c. "Recent" is a weak word in the third paragraph. You could write out that passive voice in the fourth paragraph. "JAMA" may be lost on listeners.

d. The fifth paragraph has a long relative clause ("who has covered the Missouri Legislature as part of her studies and works part-time for Columbia television station K-O-M-U") separating the subject from the verb. This would be better as a separate sentence.

3. The rewritten stories that follow are only suggestions. The objective, of course, is to teach students broadcast style.

    a. Police in Zurich, Switzerland, are looking for seven Picasso paintings. Thieves grabbed them from an art gallery over the weekend. The most famous paintings are Picasso's "Seated Woman" and "Christ of Montmartre"—both recovered from a previous theft in 1991 from a Zurich gallery.

    b. Retirement communities may have to allow youngsters to use their pools and golf courses. In this case, youngsters include people under 55. State officials in Seal Beach, California, have filed a complaint against Seal Beach Leisure World for their regulation. The rule bars even spouses under 55 from swimming in the pools and playing golf.

    c. You can save 40 percent on your holiday domestic air fares on Northwest Airlines. But move fast. You must purchase your tickets by Friday. Be sure to check the available dates. However, you can bet that other airlines will match Northwest's fares.

4. We have found this to be an excellent exercise. It encourages students to read the newspaper critically and to come up with stories that are immediate and have local interest. You may notice differences in news judgment and hold a class discussion about them. For example, what story will students choose as the lead story? In the discussion, ask students to justify their selections. Of course, the copy should be written correctly and in the best broadcast style. Your print students can benefit from the clear and simple style of broadcast writing.

Solutions to Workbook Questions and Exercises

1. See preceding exercise 1.

2. (A) a. Excellent immediacy throughout. Notice the present tense in the lead ("may have"). The second paragraph uses the present perfect ("has signed"). Look at the attributions ("say") and the present progressive in the last paragraph ("is suing").

    b. Simple conversational style. Note the contraction ("They'll") in the fifth paragraph.

    c. There doesn't seem to be any extra words.

    d. Nothing is unclear here. In the second to last paragraph, you might change the "which" clause to a separate sentence and get rid of the verb in the passive voice: "Some experts expect the service to cost $16 (M) million in the first year."

    (B) a. The present and present perfect tense are used throughout.

    b. Good contraction ("they're"). In the second sentence of the third paragraph, the "like" sounds conversational, but it is incorrect English. "Like" should be the subordinating conjunction, "as if." Note the sentence beginning with "And" in the last paragraph.

c. We might like more information. Who are the "investigators," and how many are there? The same for the "officials"; but the copy is tight.

d. Clear enough, except perhaps for what is said in point c. We might wonder too how many "other shuttles" have weak spots.

(C) a. "Continue to block" sets the tone of the story that is happening now. Note in the fourth paragraph, the attribution is "said," and in the last paragraph, it is "says."

b. Note the contraction "They've." The style is fine.

c. It's tight enough.

d. You probably have to know quite a bit of background to understand this story, but this is about all you can expect in a short report.

(D) a. Excellent use of the present in this piece.

b. Excellent conversational style. The lead is fine. Note the contractions "you've" and "it's." Compound sentences are used in the second and third paragraphs, but they sound conversational.

c. In the last paragraph, you might strike the second "have been working."

d. In the last sentence, should that be "diesel fuel" rather than just "diesel"?

(E) a. The past tense passive voice of the verbs in the third and fourth paragraphs do not connote immediacy.

b. The lead is conversational. The dash in the last paragraph also indicates a conversational style.

c. Place the fourth paragraph at the end of the story. Remove the third paragraph altogether. Rewrite the fifth paragraph as: "In a study presented today to the American College of Rheumatology, researchers looked at more than 120,000 registered nurses."

d. The rewrite in c. will help clarify. You might need to define what a "connective-tissue disease" is.

3. The rewritten stories that follow are only suggestions. The objective is to teach students broadcast style.

a. You'll be hearing weather sirens Tuesday at 10 a.m.

It's time for the annual statewide tornado drill of the National Weather Service.

If there is severe weather Tuesday, expect to hear the sirens on Thursday.

During the drill on Tuesday, a tone alert will sound on certain weather radios. It's a good time to check whether such radios are working.

The National Weather Service recommends that you take the precautions during the drill that you would take were the sirens a real warning of severe weather.

b. LOS ANGELES—Three are dead, and six are wounded in a battle over drug turf. Two are in critical condition.

Six gunmen fired on a group of 10 men Sunday night. The group was drinking beer and playing cards.

Police Chief Willie Williams says the victims were not gang members, but they were selling rock cocaine in the South Central LA neighborhood. Gang members had warned the group to stop selling at that location.

Police have made no arrests in the case.

c. BIRMINGHAM, Ala. (AP)—Another corporate executive pleads guilty.

A third former chief officer at HealthSouth Corporation agreed to plead guilty yesterday to charges arising from a widening accounting scandal.

Michael Martin was charged with conspiracy to commit wire fraud and securities fraud and with falsifying financial information. Martin was CFO from October 1997 to February 2000. He's 42 years old and lives in Birmingham.

U.S. Attorney Alice Martin said in a news conference yesterday that Martin struck a plea deal and is cooperating with authorities investigating the company.

d. Springfield police are looking for two teenagers who stabbed and robbed a 31-year-old woman Friday.

The victim was walking down an alley to the south of the 600 block of Park Avenue shortly before 11 a.m.

The teenagers stabbed the woman after she said she had no money. Then they took her money and fled west down the alley on foot.

e. Officials at the National Zoo in Washington have found a partially devoured woman's body in an outdoor lion enclosure.

A zookeeper found the unidentified woman at 7 a.m. Saturday. He coaxed the two lions back into the lion house and called police.

Police Department spokesman Sergeant Joe Gentile says the cause of death has not been established. The victim was not a zoo employee.

4. These stories have no film with them, and hence, the exercise may be for radio or television. In a normal television newscast, one or more of these stories would have a filmed report. The exercise here teaches students how to make smooth transitions from one story to the next.
    a. The lead here is OK. The wrap-up might say: "Americans might find themselves buying less and paying more."
    b. The new lead-in: "And they may find themselves eating less and gaining more. A new study suggests they're done in by their own efficiency." Keep the ending.
    c. The new lead-in: "Two teenage skinheads may find themselves with less freedom to eat what they want. They'll face charges that they murdered their parents and younger brother." After the first sentence in the fourth paragraph, you could write: "They have waived extradition from Michigan to Pennsylvania." Keep the ending.
    d. Lead-in: "Meanwhile, some abortion clinic doctors are confessing that they are afraid. They want more than handguns for protection; they're buying armored cars."

5. A. WASHINGTON (UPI)—The Forest Service today proposed a ~~policey~~ policy

of planning fires in national forest wilderness areas to reduce risk

of wildfires and to ~~permit fire too~~ permit fire to return to ~~it's~~ its natural ecological role.

R. Max Peterson, ~~cheif~~ chief of the Agriculture Department agency, says

the earlier policy of promptly suppressing all fires resulted in , in his words, "unnat-

ural accumulation of dead brush and trees in some wilderness areas."

He says permitting trained specialists to ignite and ~~mannage~~ manage fires

would permit the use of fires "to reduce unnatural fuel ~~accummula-~~ accumulations

~~tions and~~ and to allow fire once again to play its natural role in the ecology of

~~wikderness~~ wilderness ecosystems.

Under the proposed policy change, all ~~planneed~~ planned fires in ~~wilderness~~ wilderness areas

would have to be approved by a regional forester.

Peterson says a team of experts . . . including botanists, wildlife

biologists and fire and recreation managers . . . ~~woulld~~ would study each sit-

uation and make recommendations. He says the public would be

included in each decision, and the public will be asked to comment by

~~Aug.~~ August 4th on the proposed policy change.

The Forest Service administers ~~25½~~ 25 and one-half million acres of the National

Wilderness Preservation System, or about 85 ~~%~~ percent of wilderness outside of

Alaska. The rest is administered by the U.S. Department of the Interior.

B. WASHINGTON (UPI)—Scientists say people who travel or whose

work schedules are changed drastically may be able to avoid "jet lag"

and function nearly normally if they ~~got~~ get enough sleep after the

disruption.

102

A study shows loss of sleep is just as important a ~~cuase~~ cause of jet lag—the urge to sleep at inappropriate times—as the disruption of a traveler's body clock during journeys through several time zones. Thomas Roth is head of the sleep disorders center at the Henry Ford Hospital in Detroit and a co-author of the report in the journal *Science*. He says /a good part of jet lag is loss of sleep./ He adds ~~thjat~~ that is important because /historically the emphasis has been on the /time/ shift, NOT on the loss of sleep./

After two normal days, the people in the study/ conducted at Henry Ford and Stanford University went to bed at noon for ~~2~~ three days. Those who coped most successfully with the change/in hours took a short-acting prescription sedative, ~~whhich~~ which stayed in ~~there~~ their bodies ~~5 to 6~~ five to six hours. They functioned normally or nearly so.

Another group of volunteers took a longer-acting sedative and got a good sleep, but reported feeling drowsy and sluggish when ~~theyt~~ they got up. In some cases, they were drowsier than those who took a placebo—a fake drug.

The placebo group lost sleep and also had a hard time staying ~~allert~~ alert during the following ~~"day."~~ day.

The report says ~~behaviour~~ behavior of the placebo group confirmed that sleep and subsequent alertness /are significantly impaired for at least three days after a sudden 12-hour shift in the sleep-awake schedule.

C. KANSAS CITY (UPI)—A former mobster turned FBI informer today sobbed ~~uring in his ex-wife's $1 1/2 million lawsuit~~ during testimony in his ex-wife's one and one-half million dollar lawsuit against the federal

103

government . . . saying he had never taken his son with him to ~~comit~~ *commit*

crimes.

Asked by government attorney Mary Sterling whether his son had

ever accompanied him on a /score,/ Michael Ruffalo ~~Sr.~~ *Senior* cried, "I've

done a lot of things in my life. I've never taken my son on something

like that."

U.S. District Judge Howard Sachs, who is hearing the lawsuit of

Donna Ruffalo without a jury, recessed court for about 10 minutes to

allow Ruffalo to compose himself.

Mrs. Ruffalo, Michael's ex-wife, is seeking damages from the fed-

eral government for hiding her son in the federal witness protection

program with his father in 1986. The boy entered the program at age ~~9.~~ *nine.*

Ruffalo, who testified behind a ~~screan~~ *screen* under heavy guard by fed-

eral officials, said when he decided to enter the program he asked

Mike ~~Jr.~~ *Junior* what he wanted to do.

Ruffalo said, *quote,* "I asked my son if he wanted to go with me, and

never see his mother again. He said he never hardly saw her anyway."

Ruffalo said he was the ~~boys~~ *boy's* primary caretaker ~~thoughou~~ *throughout* his 14

years.

He disputed testimony given earlier in the morning by Gayle Wiser,

Mrs. Ruffalo's sister.

Mrs. Wiser said that her daughter, Evie, who is now 27, lived with

Mrs. Ruffalo for ~~aoubt 4~~ *about four* years beginning at the age of 11. Speaking of

that time in their lives, Mrs. Wiser said . . . "She'd (Evie) rather live

with her than with me." But Ruffalo said he did not think his former

104

wife gave the girl very good care. He also said he often saw Mrs. Ruffalo drunk. But Mrs. Wiser had said her sister's separation from her son caused the alcohol problem.

At the time Ruffalo entered the program, Mrs. Ruffalo had legal custody of the boy ~~threw~~ through the Jackson County Circuit Court. She subsequently filed a lawsuit in federal court seeking the return of the boy and asking for monetary damages. Sachs has ordered the government to permit ~~her 3~~ Mrs. Ruffalo three visits a year with her son.

6. This exercise demonstrates to students how different stations have different ways of doing things. They should be prepared to adapt.
7. Again, we recommend that you assign a particular day's newscast so that you can have a good class discussion. It is best to videotape the newscast to help refresh students' memories and thereby encourage class discussion.
   Discuss questions like these:

   - Was the commentary appropriate?
   - Was there too much commentary? Not enough?
   - Was the message clear at all times?

8. See the preceding exercise 4.
9. **CHALLENGE EXERCISE.** Suggestions: Emphasize biggest bank buyout; eliminate number of customers, branches and states; drop most other numbers from the lead.

CHAPTER 20: WRITING FOR ONLINE MEDIA

Overview

Writing for online media is still in its infancy. No one has begun to master this new medium, and no one knows for sure where it is taking us.

One thing we do know for sure: Writing for online media is different from writing for print, and those who shovel print onto their Web sites are making a big mistake.

This chapter begins with three important principles of writing online:

1. *The reader rules.* Readers read only what they want to read, when the want to read it and in the order in which they choose to read it.
2. *The writing is nonlinear.* Your students have been taught the importance of coherence, of outlining stories carefully, because after all, words follow words and paragraphs follow paragraphs. Writing online is more about writing in bits and chunks so that readers can find quickly what they want and only what they want.

3. *Structure is everything.* Because writing online is nonlinear, students of online writing come to think that structure is no longer important. On the contrary, structuring the story in the way the reader is most likely to want to pursue it is extremely important.

We know that online readers do not read everything; they "surf" the copy. The trick is to make them "dive," to help them find what they want as quickly and easily as possible. This chapter provides 10 ways to make divers out of surfers. Perhaps the most important thing to stress is that the Internet is about being connected. Writers no longer need to put everything in one story. They can connect to other related aspects of the story that either they or someone else has written. The important words writers should always keep in mind are "for more information, see . . ."

The chapter ends with some brief reflections on legal and ethical concerns. Obviously, the Internet will spawn dozens of books on these concerns. We are, indeed, caught in a web of legal and ethical complications.

Solutions to Textbook Questions and Exercises

1. You might actually assign the story you wish your students to pursue and which newspaper Web sites to pursue them on. You might also suggest that they follow the 10 guidelines in the chapter in assessing whether the sites use good online writing techniques.
2. You need to be sure that all of your students do not go to the same person or persons. You might expand this assignment to local magazines or local corporations, especially for those in your class who are more inclined toward a profession in magazines or in public relations.
3. It might be easier for your students if you choose a national or international story. That's not necessarily true, of course.
4. Again, you might include corporate or organization Web sites for your public relations students.

Solutions to Workbook Questions and Exercises

1. You may wish to send all of your students to the same Web site so that you can make comparisons in what they find. Doing this will also help you have a better class discussion.
2. Those who read online want to read only what they need to read, and readers are vastly different in their needs. Some will want only a brief summary of the information; others will want a short version of the story; still others will want to read as much as they can. That's what layering is all about.
3. Generally, readers do not go to the Internet to read. They go for information. You may not hold important information back from them by putting it in the fifth paragraph. Online readers are impatient. You must allow them to "click here" for the information they want when they want it and in the order in which they want it.
4. Here are some suggestions:

   - Has this happened before at this school? At other schools in the community? At other schools in the nation?

- What are schools doing about metal detectors? How have they worked? How do students react to them?
- How many deaths are the result of school shootings? How many such incidents have there been in the past 10 years?
- What were the reactions of parents of students in this school when the gun was found?
- What were the reactions of the teachers? Especially the teachers of the student who was caught with the gun?
- What were the reactions of fellow students?
- How did the student acquire the gun?
- Is it possible for a student to buy a gun in a local gun store?
- What is the reaction of the local chapter of the National Rifle Association?

5. There is, of course, no one way to write these stories online. Let's look at them separately and make a few suggestions.
   A. First, there are clearly two stories here. One is about the bill to create a state don't-call list for telemarketers; the second concerns an anti-abortion proposal that was attached to a bill about how to spend money obtained from the tobacco industry. There is even another short news story about a proposal that bans telemarketers from blocking caller-ID components on phones. Break up the stories.

   Then, write a good inverted pyramid lead or a one-paragraph summary of each of the bills.

   You also need to find some other stories on the subject to link to, both local and national.
   B. The best way to handle this meeting, which delved into so many matters, is to make a bullet list of summaries of all of the ideas expressed. In another chunk, you may want to write the quotations of the candidates regarding the ideas discussed.
6. This question assumes that most newspaper Web sites do not yet use film or sound. You may find some that already have their stories complemented with sound or film or both. It is important to discuss with your students the likelihood that journalists of the future will be required to have various media skills. They will have to know which medium tells the story most effectively and which media work together to have the most impact.
7. This matter is already hotly debated. Why would you wish to send readers to another media outlet—especially if the media are your competition? But isn't it better for you to be the reliable source of information for your readers? Wouldn't it be to your benefit if people knew that by reading your publication they would have access to a lot of pertinent and related information? Isn't it all about information and being an information provider? Certainly Nielsen seems correct in saying that readers want to know that authors have done their homework and that they have reliable sources.
8. Again, you may wish to assign the story so that you can compare different students' work and have a better class discussion.
9. This assignment should be especially pleasing to magazine students. City and regional magazines generally have useful Web sites.

10. Some newspapers are requiring reporters to prepare two stories—one for the paper and one for the Web. Often you will find that the Web version is merely a shorter version without any of the other components of good online writing. You will find that the writers rarely write in chunks, do little bulleting and even less linking.
11. Some questions are: Do the ads have an appearance similar to the editorial copy? Can they be mistaken for editorial copy? Is a distinct typeface used for the ads?

   Are the ads placed next to stories that relate to them? Does it appear that the ads were sold because there was a story on a certain subject? A most blatant example would be a story about a local winery with an ad from the winery next to it.

CHAPTER 21: WRITING FOR PUBLIC RELATIONS

Overview

Even though you may be using this text in a newswriting course, you are certainly aware that many of your students never intend to work in a news organization. Many others who may start out in news will eventually end up in some area of public relations. The stereotype of public relations students is that they want to go into the field because they like people. The fact is that they had better like writing—or at least, they had better be good at it.

This chapter begins with a discussion of the different approach public relations writers take. If you came into teaching journalism from a life as a reporter, it may be difficult for you to explain the role of the public relations professional. You may even question whether one can be ethical in such a profession. It's important for you to discuss these issues for the sake of those going into public relations as well as for those who are not.

The chapter then discusses the diversity of writing tasks those going into public relations can expect. Whether they write for clients while at a public relations firm or work for an organization and do internal and external public relations, they may be expected to write anything from annual reports to newsletters, intranet messages and memos.

Because it is one of the most important jobs a public relations person does, this chapter focuses on writing news releases. However, just as newswriting has changed and gotten "beyond the inverted pyramid," here students are urged to experiment with different approaches to the news release. Some would call it taking a "feature" approach; we prefer to think of it as merely a more compelling form of writing.

Solutions to Textbook Questions and Exercises

1. You may want to be careful not to flood one particular public relations professional with a whole host of students. You will find these professionals most cooperative, but it's probably a good idea to call them and discuss your project with them.
2. Target audiences might be the students, perhaps the fraternity of the student who was killed, faculty, alumni, family, hometown folks, high school

classmates and so on. Media might be e-mail messages, fliers, bulletin boards, campus radio, newsletters and news releases. Print materials could be developed for all of these, including scripts for campus radio.

3. Deviations from AP style:

First paragraph: In the first line, the comma goes inside the quotation marks. The time should be written "7-8:30 p.m., Wed., Oct. 22."

Third paragraph: Change "twenty-five" to a numeral.

Fourth paragraph: Abbreviate "Michigan." Also, put the commas and period inside the quotation marks.

Fifth paragraph: Change "1" to "one" and "fifty-thousand" to "50,000"; lowercase "College"; spell out "U.S."

Content a news organization might object to: In the first paragraph, remove the word "excellent." Probably you ought to get rid of "warm and engaging" in paragraph three. In the fourth paragraph, drop "superb, highly acclaimed series" or attribute it to someone. Do the same for "one of the most prestigious" in the fifth paragraph.

4. You may do this assignment in conjunction with your college or university public relations or public information office. You will be doing good public relations for your class and school.

5. This assignment accomplishes two purposes. It gets students to study the college Web site, and it makes a good topic for a news release.

Solutions to Workbook Questions and Exercises

1. Newswriters try not to have a point of view. Though they may have difficulty being objective, they should always strive to be impartial and fair.

   Public relations writers work for a client, much the same as attorneys do. They strive to tell the truth but also to present their client or their client's position from the best point of view. Often, like opinion and editorial writers, their job is to persuade.

2. You might want to make sure the same person isn't contacted by several students.

3. See textbook questions for previous exercise 2.

4. A. Errors:

First paragraph: Change "fifteen" to "15." Also, change "Over" to "More than" and abbreviate "November."

Third paragraph: Change "one million" to "1 million."

Fourth paragraph: Insert the article "the" before "American Bankers Association." Remove the hyphen from "non-profit." In the last sentence, "refaced" should be changed to "reached."

Fifth paragraph: Place the attribution at the end of the first sentence of the direct quotation, and make it "Hudson says."

Last paragraph: Change "fifteen" to the numeral; change "3" to "three."

Newsworthiness and effectiveness: In a small- to medium-sized town, this release could be good news to parents who worry about their children not reading enough. It's obviously good public relations for the bank, but that's OK because the bank is doing a worthwhile community service.

Facts to check: You might want to check all of this with the principal at Grant Elementary School. Always check the spelling of people's names (Kim Hudson) and their positions. Check the founding date (1984) and the number and nature of the national awards.

B. Errors:

First paragraph: Change "childrens'" to "children's." Hyphenate "college funding."

Second paragraph: Change "over" to "more than" in two places. Place the attribution after the first sentence of the direct quotation. Hyphenate "college funding" in the attribution. The compound "need-based" should have single quotes. Spell out "percent." Put a comma at the end of the quotation before the quotation marks.

Third paragraph: Take out the three periods that follow the first sentence. Add a comma after "example."

Fourth paragraph: Hyphenate "college funding" in both places where it occurs. The first words of the quote should be changed to "If parents have only . . ."; add commas after "forms" and "savings." Add an apostrophe after "parents." Add quotation marks at the end of the paragraph.

Fifth paragraph: Drop the first sentence.

Newsworthiness and effectiveness: The release should interest parents facing high college costs for their children.

Facts to check: You might want to check the credentials and references of Jim Burt. Also, you should check the numbers in the second paragraph.

C. Errors:

First paragraph: Insert the verb "is" ("One reason is that bathroom . . ."). Take out the comma after "sink."

Second paragraph: Insert the word "how" after "but." Add a comma after "adults." Insert the verb "offers" after "Food and Drug Administration." Use the postal service abbreviation "CO" in the address.

Third paragraph: Insert a comma after "warm." Take out the hyphen in "non-prescription."

Fourth paragraph: Take out the hyphen in "non-aspirin."

Fifth paragraph: Spell out the number "6."

Sixth paragraph: Spell out "6."

Seventh paragraph: Delete comma after "consistency." Change "rise" to "rinse."

Last paragraph: Add a comma after "(free)."

Newsworthiness and effectiveness: The release should be of interest to many people. Most newspapers have sections devoted to health and safety, and many magazines have the same. The copy could be cut somewhat, but it's quite a good piece.

Facts to check: You might want to check some of this information with a local pharmacist.

5. a. You might find a child who has participated in this program. A second choice might be to do a story about a teacher who works in the program.

  b. Again, find a college student who thought she was unable to get funding but through getting the right advice was able to find financial assistance. Parents of such a student would also make a more interesting story than what is described in this news release.

c. Here's a chance to do some real service journalism with a good graphic of a medicine cabinet and other charts. Add some "do and don't" lists, give addresses and Web sites for more information, tell readers what they should store and where. Then find a person who as a child overdosed on medicine. You might consider a contest. Have people send in the oldest label they can find in their medicine cabinet. If theirs is the oldest sent in, they win a prize!

6. Most good public-relations work is done over a period of time in a campaign that involves long-term planning and several media. It's important that your students become familiar with how this is done.

7. **CHALLENGE EXERCISE.** The point here is to make it clear that writing for radio is different from writing for print and that you should not send the same release to both media. Of course, your students may not have any experience in writing for radio and television at this point in the semester.

PART EIGHT: RIGHTS AND RESPONSIBILITIES

CHAPTER 22: MEDIA LAW

Overview

This chapter is intended to give students some basic facts about the three most important areas of communications law—libel, privacy and protection of sources.

Libel is damage to an individual's reputation, and *privacy* is the right to be left alone. Once students understand this much, they should be required to read stories in newspapers and newsmagazines, watch television and listen to radio broadcasts in order to discern possible libelous words and phrases and to see if stories or pictures are invasions of someone's right to be left alone.

The goal is to get students to realize how often libel and/or invasion of privacy issues arise. This process will allow students to see possible defenses for the various stories that are written daily.

As to the protection of sources and notes, you can keep this material up to date by having students read *Editor & Publisher* and *Broadcasting* magazines because there will be continuing activity on press-court relations. The cases in this chapter on protection of sources and notes are recent and noteworthy and will be referred to in stories students will be reading for many years.

Solutions to Textbook Questions and Exercises

1. Any lawyer would first use the defense of truth, which is an absolute form of defense. Privilege and fair comment and criticism are not applicable in this case. The jury found that *Time* could not establish that the passage in question was true. Therefore, the magazine was forced to rely on the actual malice rule. Because Sharon's attorneys could not establish that *Time* acted with malice, the magazine escaped. It is essential for students to understand that only truth is an acceptable reason for publishing or not publishing a particular passage. The news media are charged with presenting *facts*, not fiction or rumors.

2. *The New York Times* vs. Sullivan case is perhaps the most important in the history of libel law. It probably has greatly reduced the number of libel suits brought to trial and certainly has reduced the number of cases the press has lost. Because this decision places the burden on the plaintiff to establish that the newspaper, magazine or broadcast station acted with actual malice, it is of inestimable value for the media.

3. The key here is the phrase "without permission." The press has no right to trespass, and it is conceivable that the photographer in question could be guilty of that crime. Newspapers should not be in the business of gathering information illegally. Some editors would argue, using situation ethics as a defense, that if society would be well-served by publishing the pictures, the newspaper should do so. So, while the act of taking pictures on private property without permission is illegal, a question of ethics also is involved.

4. The Richmond Newspapers cases will probably be cited in all cases dealing with openness of criminal court proceedings. See, for instance,

Press Enterprise Co. vs. Superior Court of California, decided by the U.S. Supreme Court in 1984, and Press-Enterprise Co. vs. Superior Court of California, decided by the U.S. Supreme Court in 1986.

Solutions to Workbook Questions and Exercises

1. a. The protection is provided by the First Amendment, which states, in part, "Congress shall make no law . . . abridging the freedom of . . . the press."
    b. "To assure the unfettered interchange of ideas for bringing about the political and social changes desired by the people."
    c. On the federal level, there is the Freedom of Information Act passed by Congress in 1966 and amended in 1974. All 50 states have similar open record laws.
2. a. *Libel* is damage to a person's reputation caused by exposing that person to hatred, contempt or ridicule in the eyes of a substantial and respectable group.
    b. The areas are:
        1. Accusing someone of a crime.
        2. Damaging a person in his or her public office or occupation.
        3. Accusing a person of serious immorality.
        4. Reporting that someone has a loathsome (contagious or venereal) disease.
    c. Truth, privilege, and fair comment and criticism.
    d. Absolute privilege.
3. Your report must present full, fair and accurate coverage of the court session, the legislative session or the presidential press conference.
4. You will be covered if you do not misstate facts on which you base your comments or criticism.
5. a. The actual malice test was applied. To be convicted of actual malice, you must have had knowledge that what you printed or broadcast was false or you must have been reckless in disregarding whether or not the report was false.
    b. There was no actual malice in the Walker case because "hot news" was involved: The AP had a reporter on the scene of a newsworthy event. There was actual malice in the Butts case because it was not "hot news" and the information came from a conversation that was overheard by an individual who was on probation for committing a crime. In addition, no one checked game films or the source's notes, and there was no football expert assigned to the story.
    c. A *public official* is a government employee who has, or appears to the public to have, substantial responsibility for or control over the conduct of governmental affairs.
    d. One kind of public figure is a person who has assumed a role of special prominence in the affairs of society—someone who has pervasive power and influence in a community. The other kind is a person who has thrust himself or herself into the forefront of a particular public controversy in order to influence the resolution of the issues involved.
6. A reporter may be risking an invasion of privacy suit by physically intruding into a private area to get a story or a picture.

7. This involves the third possible privacy problem, in that something has been disclosed about the woman's private affairs that is true but would also be offensive to individuals of ordinary sensibilities. The press usually wins these cases.

8. If the story focuses only on what the reporter saw in the nightclub, there is no need for any additional information. However, if the piece is about the mayor as an alcoholic, more than just the word of two council members (who may be adversaries of the mayor) is needed. Some sort of medical or legal records should be secured at a minimum.

9. The first sentence in the fifth paragraph is potentially libelous. The passage implies that Payne was careless when he pulled the plug. That may be the case, but unless you can prove he was careless, do not publish this quotation. The burden on the reporter and the newspaper is to prove the accusation is true, not merely to prove that someone said it.

10. This story is potentially libelous in two of the four major areas of libel. It says that the faculty member is not doing his job appropriately and accuses him of engaging in immoral activity of a sexual nature. If the allegations are false or unprovable, the newspaper is republishing a libel even if the accuser is quoted correctly.

    If the accuser files a complaint with the court, the newspaper could base a story on a full and accurate report of the complaint. However, if the complaint is filed with the university or a state agency, and if the university or agency procedure keeps the complaint confidential during the grievance process, there would not be a privilege to report from the complaint, even if the newspaper was able to obtain a copy of the complaint.

    If there is no way for the newspaper to corroborate the allegations by talking to witnesses, there is no story yet.

11. The story contains sources who are calling the provost a liar. If this account is wrong, it is libelous.

    There is internal corroboration. An administrator and a faculty member both say that the faculty do not trust the provost. Two faculty members agree with Mary Barnridge.

    An editor would want to know whether the anonymous sources would be willing to testify in court on behalf of the newspaper. The editor would also want to know if the "sources" who have told the newspaper that the provost has been asked to resign would have reason to know for a fact that the resignation has been requested. They may simply be passing on information to the reporter that they had picked up around campus.

    If the sources are credible, this story could be printed. If it turns out to be wrong and the provost sues, the newspaper would probably need the anonymous sources to come forward. One of the key defense points would be that the information about the provost losing the trust of the faculty was an accurate representation of the faculty members' opinions.

12. If the curators did not vote to fire the chancellor, the story would be libelous. However, if it is accurate, there is no legal problem. In either case, the newspaper would not be held responsible for anyone's breach of confidentiality in talking to the newspaper.

13. The story is fine until the next-to-last paragraph when Commissioner Cummings accuses Bill Rodgers of being a fool. Unless you want to be forced to prove in court that Rodgers is a fool, delete that quotation. The meaning of the term is imprecise, and proving truth would be difficult. Rodgers may not be a public official because he is not elected, but he certainly is a public figure, having authored a proposed controversial ordinance. Nevertheless, it is unwise to print such irresponsible quotations.

14. There are no apparent legal problems in this story.

15. Here is one way the story could be written:

The city has accused a landlord of violating the city's rental housing licensing ordinance for the first time since the ordinance went into effect in January.

Prosecutor Mel Cross said Monday that Mark Dillow, 43, of 209 Perch Lane, has been charged with violating the ordinance, which requires the inspection and licensing of rental housing to ensure that minimal standards of safety are met.

City inspectors, acting on a complaint from tenant John Bowers, 21, of 303A Court Drive, found that the apartment was not licensed for rental and had not been inspected. An inspection revealed 17 fire and safety violations in Bowers' apartment alone.

Three other units in the building were not inspected, but the city has informed Dillow it plans to do so next week.

Richard Laventhol, a city housing inspector, said, "I've never seen so many violations in one spot. There were frayed electrical wires, leaky toilets, you name it. The place was disgusting."

Cross said the case will be heard in Municipal Court Monday. Dillow will be defended by attorney Joan Anderson.

Conviction is punishable with a fine of up to $1,000 and six months in jail.

16. Regardless of whether you see a copyright notice, the article would be protected by copyright. You need permission to reprint. However, if you are using the facts to write a story, you do not need permission.

17. There is probably no legal problem with this story. The public administrator is a public official, and her actions are subject to public review and scrutiny. The fairness question is another issue. The fairness of the story may depend in large part on how prominently it is played. If it occupies a banner across the top of page one, it probably has been blown out of proportion because the administrator is not gaining personally from the transaction—at least not to any measurable extent. It may be that the administrator did this not with the intent of making money, but because keeping all the accounts in one bank is more convenient. An interview with the administrator is essential. That should give you a clue about how to proceed.

18. **CHALLENGE EXERCISE.** A lawyer representing Gene Gotti and John Carneglia, both convicted mobsters, asked for the names of the jurors. He said that he wanted to question them about the reason for the dismissal of the 12th juror, who had told the judge he had been threatened by two strangers. (See *Newsday*, April 22, 1994.)

A newspaper could face legal problems for printing the names of jurors under developing negligence law. If any of the jurors were later harmed, the newspaper could be held responsible.

CHAPTER 23: ETHICS

Overview

We are sure you do not need to be persuaded about the importance of introducing students to the ethical problems facing journalists. When we first proposed this book, we placed the discussion of ethics among the beginning chapters to demonstrate how important we thought it was.

The plan proved to be impractical. Until students have had some exposure to journalism and the kinds of stories journalists do, it just doesn't make sense to talk in theoretical terms about ethics.

Nevertheless, it would be equally impractical and pedagogically absurd to wait until the course is over to introduce this chapter. We will leave the timing of its introduction up to you.

You may wish to set aside a certain amount of time each week for a discussion and debate about some ethical problem facing journalists. Far too often, however, these discussions become nothing more than an expression of uninformed opinions or of gut feelings as to what is right and wrong.

Granted, different people may solve ethical issues in different ways. Nevertheless, students and practitioners should be able to discuss the underlying principles on which they have based their decisions.

In this chapter, we not only discuss some ethical principles, but we also provide a framework for working through ethical or principled reasoning. We have borrowed the Potter Box as a means to reach ethical decisions. You will find that the Potter Box also provides a framework that will give order to class discussion of these issues.

You may wish to study the Potter Box further in *Media Ethics, Cases and Moral Reasoning* by Christians et al. (See Suggested Readings in Chapter 23 of the textbook.) Of course, you may also wish to study other books on ethical theory. The dangers in discussions of ethics are that we may oversimplify issues, we may act as if there is only one way to be ethical, or we may act as if there are no ethical principles at all and that everything is completely relative.

However, if we strike a balance and help students begin to do principled reasoning, everyone benefits—the students, the field of journalism and, ultimately, society itself.

Solutions to Textbook Questions and Exercises

1. Even deontologists have a problem here. If as journalists they believe that it is their duty to report the news regardless, they would run the story. If they believe that the protection of the child's life is an absolute, they would feel they have a duty not to do so. The teleologists would have less trouble not running the story. If the purpose here is to save the life of the

child, any means could be used to do so. Situation ethicists could come down on either side of the case. Certainly, love of neighbor would indicate that the child's life should not be endangered.

2. Absolutists might conclude that any acceptance of a freebie is unethical. Teleologists might argue that readers are better served by the reporting of such a travel story. If it were the only way the news organization could afford to cover it, the acceptance of a free trip might be ethical. It might become more acceptable if the writer informed the public that he or she accepted the free trip. Situationists would apply similar thinking.

3. Photographers who have been caught in these situations have chosen all of these options. If first at the scene, most photographers would call the office or tell someone to send the police. However, from that point on, what should be done is open for serious debate. Deontologists could argue that the photographer's job is to take pictures. Or they could argue that the photographer's first job is to preserve human life. Would the photographer's mere presence add to the possibility of the man's jumping off the bridge? In the extreme, Ayn Rand's rational self-interest would dictate that the photographer do whatever it takes to get good pictures to further his or her career.

4. The question here involves the use of deceit to get a story. The issue seems serious enough to be of profound public importance. Individuals are being harmed. Has the editor exhausted all other alternatives? Are the news media the only means of correcting the situation? Will the editor give full disclosure of the deception and the reason for it? What will be the impact on the credibility of the paper?

5. a. *The situation.* You'd need to do some more reporting on the situation. Be sure of all the facts. Has the minister ever disclosed the fact that his son was conceived out of wedlock? Has he a public record of condemning premarital sex?

   b. *Values.* Religion is a value in our society. Would this harm not just this minister but all ministers and religion? One could argue that religion itself has a value of confession and forgiveness. Truth certainly is a value, especially for a minister. Yet a person's good name and reputation are also highly valued. Does this incident reflect the kind of person the minister is 18 years later? Does this have anything to do with whether he would make a good mayor?

   c. *Principles.* Deontologists who believe that it is the duty of journalists to report the news would not hesitate to publish or broadcast the story. Besides, they would argue, if their audience found out that they were concealing this information, they might lose trust in the news organization.

   Love of neighbor might keep some from doing the story. However, utilitarianism might dictate that in the long run, for the good of all, society is better served by knowing all there is to know about a political candidate. Report it, and let the public decide whether it wants to elect this person.

   Pragmatic considerations or rational self-interest would dictate that you not pass up what would be a good story. It could sell papers or increase the ratings. It might even win a prize.

117

d. *Loyalties.* Loyalty to your readers might mean that you owe it to them to tell the story. Loyalty to your stockholders might indicate the same.

e. *Decision.* It's a tough call. Many journalists would do the story.

6. As all of the literature suggests, this is not a simple question. You'll get a great class discussion from this one.

Solutions to Workbook Questions and Exercises

1. a. See the response to the preceding exercise 1. The situation is essentially the same.

b. Absolutists would do the story. People should know that they are in danger, and they should know that the police are not protecting the merchants. There are other options. The merchants can contract with services, such as Brinks, to pick up the receipts. In some communities, the police escort merchants carrying receipts. The merchants could get together and hire an armed guard. Perhaps they should.

2. It would be misleading and even harmful to present "answers" to all of the following cases. Obviously, there are no clear answers. What these cases demand is some ethical or principled reasoning, and using the Potter Box enables journalists to do that.

Students may object to this whole process. We have heard them say that people can choose any principles they like to reach the decision they want to reach. Of course, that's true. People are free to be unethical and to do no reasoning at all. But this "method" assumes that one is serious about wishing to reach an ethical decision.

Yes, depending on the ethical principles chosen, you may come to different conclusions. Unless you are an absolutist, that is inevitable. Even if you embrace John Merrill's deontelics or Edmund Lambeth's mixed-rule deontology, there is nothing that indicates that you will reach the same conclusion as someone else using those principles.

Some principles apply better to the situation at hand. Perhaps those principles or a single principle will be the most influential in reaching a decision. Certainly you do not reach a decision based on a score (five for and four against—therefore, do it).

Remember, too, that principled reasoning never stops. You bring one decision into another, you reconsider, you even change your mind. Your ethical decision making gets better the more you practice it.

And most assuredly, it becomes easier and takes less time. That's why saying the Potter Box is useless because it is too time-consuming is so facetious. As you acquire any habit, good or bad, virtue or vice, that habit becomes easy and natural.

We are presenting an examination here of situation "a" as an example of how the various ethical situations outlined in this exercise might be solved. We leave it to you and to your students to wrestle your way in and around the box.

One more thing. You don't have to go "around" the box. You can go from box to box in any order and then back again. The box serves only to give structure to your reasoning process.

a. *Situation:* Again, do some more reporting. How close are we to elections? How serious are these charges? How reliable are the sources?
Values: The values in all of these cases remain about the same. We
value a free press, we value the press as a watchdog of government,
we value presenting the best available version of the truth, we value
people's reputations and their right to privacy, we value property
rights and the right to a good living, we value equal opportunity and
equal protection under the law.
Principles:
(1) Kant's categorical imperative would demand that you never do
damage to a person's reputation—without at least being able to
prove it beyond a shadow of a doubt.
(2) Love of neighbor might demand that you do no harm to this candidate, or at least that you do the harm only out of love for others.
You are never ethical if you are out to get someone or to inflict
needless harm.
(3) On the one hand, utilitarianism might demand that the greatest
good for the greatest number means you publish the story. On the
other hand, if the claims go unproved, the public loses faith in the
news media and serious harm is done. And what if the public finds
out that you had these four sources saying these things and reported nothing?
(4) If you used Rawls' veil of ignorance, you would be more likely not
to run the story. You would not run a story of an average citizen
being accused anonymously of certain charges, so why would you
run an unsubstantiated story about a candidate for governor? Everyone is the same under the veil.
As a separate item, running the names of those who asked to be
anonymous would be an ethical violation for most journalists—
except for antinomians and for those who think anything is legitimate for the sake of a good story.
Loyalties: Owners and stockholders would be happy with a story that
sold newspapers or made the ratings go up. Loyalty to readers might
lead you to publish the story. Most certainly loyalty to readers would
demand that you pursue the story vigorously.
Judgment: Most journalists would not run the story. If the four sources
turn out to have a vendetta against the candidate, too much harm is
done to everyone. You need some verifiable information and a couple
of sources who will go on the record.
3. Good ethical practice would demand that you credit the written source
for the quotes. Moreover, copyright also demands it, so you may get into
trouble with the law if you do not credit the source.
4. Most students will agree that their news organization should have a code
of ethics. Such a code may set limits and guidelines that should help journalists form their own set of standards. The more difficult question is
one of enforcement. Some news organizations suspend staff without pay
for certain infringements such as plagiarism. Obviously, some staff have
been fired. News organizations need to spell out the procedures for such
enforcement.

5. The answers to this question will, of course, be numerous and varied. This is a good exercise to introduce for class discussion.
6. **CHALLENGE EXERCISE.** Reading codes of ethics can be instructive, both for the specific content and for all of the vague statements you find. Reading such codes should help students gather information that will help them set up their own code of ethics. In the end, that is the only way a person can be ethical.

APPENDIX 1: TWENTY COMMON ERRORS OF GRAMMAR AND PUNCTUATION

Punctuation Exercises (I)

1. The account executive/ who was wearing a blue suit/ was a Harvard graduate.

   Take out the commas. The relative clause is restrictive (necessary) to understand who was a Harvard graduate. Commas around words, phrases and clauses indicate that the words can be taken out without changing or losing the meaning of the sentence.

2. His wife/ Denise/ was in her 40s but she acted like a 10 year old.

   Take out the commas around "Denise" (we assume he has only one wife). Put a comma after "40s" (compound sentence with a coordinating conjunction). Put hyphens between "10" and "year" and "year" and "old."

3. Her secretary, Helen, and her executive assistant Bob accompanied her.

   This sentence could be punctuated correctly if we assume that she has several secretaries and only one executive assistant.

4. The third office which has green drapes is Tom's.

   If we use "which," there must be commas around the relative clause. That means it is indeed the third office. If we change the "which" to "that," we use no commas. That means it is not the third office but the third office that has green drapes.

5. The short stocky muscular/ young man was no member of the middle class.

   We need commas after "short" and "stocky," but not between "muscular" and "young." You can put an "and" between "short" and "stocky" but not between "muscular" and "young." When you can place an "and" between adjectives or when you can reverse them, that means the adjectives are coordinate—they modify the noun equally. When they do, you must place a comma between them.

6. The broken/ old man drank all alone in the smelly/ pink bar.

   No commas. "Old" and "pink" are not coordinate adjectives. Adjectives that refer to color, shape, age, material or nationality are not coordinate. They always relate more closely to the nouns they modify.

7. If employees care enough they will give an all out effort.

   You must have a comma after the introductory subordinate clause in this complex sentence and hyphenate "all-out."

8. Nodding to him to come she smiled congenially.

   You must have a comma after the introductory participial phrase.

9. The tall newly constructed building is unsafe.

   Put a comma between the adjectives. Remove the hyphen; never hyphenate adverbs ending in "ly."

10. Because she knew the company well she trusted its products.

    Place a comma after the introductory subordinate clause.

11. The age old truism took a strange new twist.

    Place a hyphen between "age" and "old" and a comma between "strange" and "new."

12. The friendly looking dog did not bother anyone.

    "Friendly" is an adjective, not an adverb, and here "friendly-looking" is a compound modifier.

13. The weak unsteady desk was poorly constructed.

    Put a comma between "weak" and "unsteady," and take out the hyphen ("ly" adverb).

14. The computer ~~which~~ *that* had just been repaired was destroyed in a fire.

    The relative clause is restrictive, necessary, to know which computer had been destroyed by fire. Change the "which" to "that."

15. The limousine had turned left and he could no longer see it.

    Put a comma before the coordinating conjunction "and" in the compound sentence.

16. He was old-fashioned but he was not closed minded.

    Put a comma before the coordinating conjunction "but" in the compound sentence. You need to hyphenate "closed-minded."

17. The tall brick house stood in a neatly kept lot.

    No comma is needed between "tall" and "brick" ("brick" is a material). Take out the hyphen between "neatly" and "kept" ("ly" adverb).

18. He never liked being interviewed and often refused to see reporters.

    Take out the comma before the "and." This is not a compound sentence. The sentence has a compound predicate. Never separate two predicates (or subjects) with a comma.

19. Playing the game well was important to her.

    Take out the comma after the gerundive phrase. The phrase is the subject of the sentence. Never put a comma between the subject of a sentence and the verb.

20. At the time of the murder she was out of town.

    Place a comma after long prepositional phrases and after two or more prepositional phrases as is the case here.

122

Punctuation Exercises (II)

1. Although he worked hard, he pleased few people.
   Always place a comma after an introductory clause.

2. The children in the room, and their parents who stood by them, were completely silent.
   Take out the comma after "room" (compound subject), and remove the comma after "them."

3. The association was growing; the staff was not.
   Never join two sentences with a comma. Here a semicolon indicates the two thoughts are closely related.

4. She tried using the copier, but was unsuccessful.
   Remove the comma. This is not a compound sentence.

5. Working through the night, she finished the job.
   Put a comma after "night." Always place a comma after an introductory participial phrase.

6. After she completed the exam, she left town.
   Place a comma after "exam." Always put a comma after an introductory clause.

7. Instead of going to the library, she took a nap.
   Put a comma after two or more introductory prepositional phrases.

8. Bill studied hard; nevertheless, he failed the test.
   You need a semicolon after "hard." "Nevertheless" is not a coordinating conjunction but a conjunctive adverb. You may, of course, break this into two sentences.

9. Generally, students who miss class regularly, are unhappy with the professor.
   No punctuation is necessary. You can place a comma after introductory adverbs, but it is not necessary. The relative clause is restrictive, necessary, to tell us which students you are talking about.

10. The time was up, so the points did not count.
    You need a comma after "up" because this is a compound sentence, and "so" is a coordinating conjunction.

11. The facilities, equipment, and personnel were excellent.
    Remove the comma after "equipment." Do not place a comma before the "and" or the "or" in a series unless the meaning is unclear. This is an Associated Press rule.

123

12. Unless you feel qualified‸ you should not apply.

    You need a comma after the introductory clause.

13. You did not come͡ because you felt you were not wanted.

    Remove the comma after "come." You do not need to place a comma before a subordinate clause that follows an independent clause.

14. The rains came‸ and they did not stop for three days.

    You need a comma before the coordinating conjunction "and" in this compound sentence.

15. The woman͡ who is wearing the mink coat͡ is his wife.

    No commas are needed. The relative clause is restrictive, necessary, to know which woman was his wife. You could argue that this is true only if there is more than one woman involved. However, the definite article "the" indicates that there is more than one woman.

16. Playing with a broken thumb‸ Tom failed to score.

    Place a comma after the introductory participial phrase.

17. The heavy‸equipment dealer also had a small farm income.

    You probably need a hyphen between "heavy" and "equipment" unless you are writing about an overweight equipment dealer. We don't know whether to put a hyphen between "small" and "farm." Are you talking about income from a small farm or a farm's income that is small?

18. The weary͡ old man walked slowly along the long‸dusty road.

    Do not put a comma between "weary" and "old" ("old" refers to age), but do put one between "long" and "dusty."

19. Tom, Bill and I are not going.

    The sentence needs no comma after "Bill," according to Associated Press style. It is interesting that "Tom" could be direct address.

20. Walking in the rain without an umbrella͡ can be therapeutic.

    Remove the comma after "umbrella." Don't put a comma between the subject of the sentence and the verb.

Punctuation Exercises (III)

1. The tall͡ square building will be torn down.

    No comma is necessary ("square" refers to shape).

2. The woman͡ who was eating the cherry pie͡ is a surgeon.

    Remove the commas. The relative clause is restrictive.

3. The thin balding middle-aged man is the president.

   Place a comma between "thin" and "balding," but not between "balding" and "middle-aged" (refers to age).

4. Because she was economy-minded she bought the small one.

   Put a comma after the introductory clause.

5. His father was old fashioned but he loved MTV.

   You need to hyphenate "old-fashioned" and to put a comma before the coordinating conjunction, "but," in this compound sentence.

6. He left his middle class neighborhood but he lost none of his middle class values.

   Place a hyphen between both uses of "middle-class," and put a comma before "but"—a coordinating conjunction in this compound sentence.

7. The properly trained secretary knew about nonrestrictive clauses.

   Remove the hyphen between "properly" and "trained" ("ly" adverb), and no hyphen is needed in "nonrestrictive." See Associated Press Stylebook.

8. The company ~~which~~ that had the better benefit package was her obvious choice.

   The relative clause is restrictive, necessary, to know which company she chose; change the "which" to "that."

9. The expensive blue tie appealed to the dapper young executive.

   No hyphens are necessary. "Blue" is a color, and "young" refers to age.

10. The canary yellow hat did not go with the heavy blue coat.

    You need a hyphen between "canary" and "yellow" but not between "heavy" and "blue" (refers to color).

11. Before she worked here she worked there.

    Place a comma after the introductory dependent clause.

12. He tried hard yet he seldom succeeded.

    Place a comma before "yet," which is a coordinating conjunction in this compound sentence.

13. She knew he would go it was just a matter of time.

    Do not join two sentences with a comma. Here the thoughts are closely related, so join them with a semicolon.

14. If I come I will not wear a tie.

    Put a comma after the introductory dependent clause.

15. What I need$\wedge$ is a long vacation.

    Remove the comma after "what I need"; this noun clause is the subject of the sentence.

16. Work proceeded nicely$\wedge$ and no one seemed to notice.

    Never use a semicolon followed by a coordinating conjunction. Put a comma before the "and" in this compound sentence; or remove the "and," and put in a semicolon.

17. I was in charge$\wedge$ and I accept full responsibility.

    Put a comma before the "and" in this compound sentence.

18. She succeeded$\wedge$ because she was immensely capable.

    Take out the comma before the subordinating conjunction that follows the independent clause.

19. William did little work$\wedge$ but he always seemed busy.

    Place a comma before "but," a coordinating conjunction in this compound sentence.

20. No one on the magazine staff agreed$\wedge$ therefore, the plan failed.

    You need a semicolon before "therefore," which is a conjunctive adverb, not a coordinating conjunction. You may also break this into two sentences.

Pronoun Exercises

1. He took Tim and ~~I~~ *me* to the movie.

    The pronoun must be in the objective case because it is the direct object of the verb.

2. Between you and ~~I~~ *me* pronouns can be difficult to use correctly.

    The pronoun must be in the objective case because it is the object of the preposition.

3. He was the young man ~~that~~ *who* caught the foul ball.

    Don't call a person a "that."

4. He did not know ~~who~~ *whom* to ask.

    "Who" must be in the objective case here because it is the subject of the infinitive.

5. A writer must always check his sources.

    Avoid sexism. Better to write the sentence: "Writers must always check their sources." Or: "If you are a writer, you must always check your sources."

6. The professor spoke to Jill and ~~I~~ [*me*] just last week.

   The pronoun must be in the objective case because it is the indirect object of the verb.

7. Who~~m~~ [*Who*] do you think cheated on the exam?

   "Who" is the subject of the sentence. The words "do you think" are parenthetical.

8. Most people ~~that~~ [*who*] work at home are happier than those who don't.

   Do not refer to people as "that."

9. Instead of ~~he~~ [*him*] and ~~I~~ [*me*], he chose ~~she~~ [*her*] and Sheri.

   "Him" and "me" are objects of a preposition and must be in the objective case. "She" must be changed to "her" because the pronoun is the direct object of the verb.

10. The corporation guaranteed all of ~~their~~ [*its*] products.

    "Corporation" is singular, and therefore "their" must be changed to "its."

11. Everybody wishes they could write well.

    "Everybody" is always singular. Pronouns must agree with their antecedent in number, gender and case. You could write: "All people wish they could write well."

12. It is ~~me~~ [*I*] who should take the blame.

    The linking verb "is" can never be followed by an object. The pronoun must be in subjective or nominative case.

13. It was not who~~m~~ you think it was.

    Don't use the objective case after an intransitive, linking verb.

14. Each student brought their own lunch.

    The antecedent "student" is singular. The pronouns must be single. Better to write it: "All the students brought their own lunch." Or: "Each student brought lunch."

15. The group is having ~~their~~ [*its*] meeting this morning.

    "Group" is singular, and the pronoun referring to it cannot be plural.

16. An architect should never publicize his fees.

    Avoid sexism. Better: "Architects should never publicize their fees." Or: "An architect should never publicize fees." Or: "If you are an architect, never publicize your fees."

17. She walked right behind Bill and ~~I~~ [*me*].

    Objects of prepositions must be in the objective case.

127

18. Whom are you talking about?

"Whom" is the object of the preposition "about." Better to write it: "About whom are you talking?" Some say never end a sentence with a preposition.

19. ~~A criminal~~ *Criminals* must pay for their crimes.

The antecedent "criminal" is singular; therefore, the pronoun that refers to it must be singular. Better to write it: "Criminals must pay for their crimes."

20. Is that ~~her~~ *she* coming down the hall?

You must use the subjective case after the linking or intransitive verb "is."

Exercises with Other Grammatical Problems

1. If I ~~was~~ *were* you, I wouldn't go.

You must use the subjunctive mood of the verb here because "if" introduces a clause that is contrary to fact.

2. The motion on the floor if passed ~~will~~ *would* stop debate.

The "motion" is not yet passed, so we need the conditional subjunctive "would" rather than the indicative "will."

3. ~~She's~~ *She has* often gone to the library on Tuesdays.

Do not use "has" or "have" as a contraction. You may say "he's handsome."

4. He suddenly left the room saying he was tired of questions.

The "room" was not doing the saying here. The participle is dangling. Better to write two sentences or to write the sentence: "Saying he was tired of questions, he suddenly left the room."

5. Playing baseball in the park, *he injured* his left leg ~~was injured~~.

"His left leg" was not "playing baseball." The sentence begins with a dangling participle.

6. He ⌐only⌐ did that ⌐one time.

The adverb "only" is misplaced.

7. She ridiculed the student *who was* in her class with the spiked hair.

The class did not have spiked hair.

8. Maurice and all his friends like͜s hotdogs.

Compound subjects must have plural verbs.

9. If that ~~was~~ *were* the case, he would still be in office.

The condition is not a fact; therefore, the verb must be in the subjunctive mood.

128

10. Working through the night, *he began to have an ache in* his back ~~began to ache~~.

His "back" was not "working through the night." The sentence begins with a dangling participle. The subject of the introductory participial phrase must be the same as the subject of the sentence.

11. He only worked at the magazine for six months.

The adverb "only" is misplaced.

12. To be successful, *you must have* good work habits ~~are necessary~~.

"Good work habits" cannot be successful. The introductory infinitive phrase must have the same subject as the subject of the sentence.

13. If I *were* ~~was~~ there, I surely would remember.

A condition contrary to fact must have the verb in the subjunctive mood.

14. Bill, along with all of his buddies, *loves* ~~love~~ to dance.

"Bill," the subject of the verb, is singular and must have a singular verb. The prepositional phrase does not determine the number of the verb.

15. The proposed constitutional amendment ~~will~~ *would* ban gay marriage.

The "amendment" is not a fact and therefore neither is the result. The verb must be in the conditional subjunctive, not in the indicative.

16. She likes the park in Springfield that has a mile-long running track.

It's a confusing sentence. Rewrite it: "The park in Springfield that she likes has a mile-long track."

17. Mary and those who think like her ~~is~~ *are* often wrong.

Compound subjects demand a plural verb.

(l. c.) 18. He hurried down the hall saying he was late.

The hall was not "saying." Participial phrases must run into the nouns they modify or follow directly after them.

19. If he ~~was~~ *were* really drunk, he would not be speaking so clearly.

The verb must be in the subjunctive mood because the condition is not a fact.

20. He only did these exercises because he was required to do them.

The adverb "only" is misplaced.

APPENDIX 2: WIRE SERVICE STYLE SUMMARY

Most editors insist that reporters have a working knowledge of style. This appendix is designed to familiarize students with the key points of wire service style used by most daily newspapers.

It is a good idea to explain to students that style rules are established for the purpose of ensuring consistency within the newspaper. Most editors agree that any style rule can be violated if there is a good reason to do so. Sometimes there is. Nevertheless, consistency is most easily established when there are guidelines for handling common items in the newspaper. The AP and UPI stylebooks are written with that purpose in mind.

It is also a good idea to emphasize that most newspapers will establish exceptions to wire service style. For example, the wire services call for numbered street names to be handled this way: First Street, Second Street and so on, but use numerals for 10 and above, as 11th Street, 31st Street and so on. In a town with only 10 numbered streets, it might make sense for the local paper to use Tenth Street; that would make the style consistent with that used for the other nine. There may be many such reasons for creating exceptions to wire service style.

Some newspapers also write supplements for the wire service stylebooks to establish consistency in writing about local institutions, places and events.

The two major wire services have written their stylebooks as alphabetized reference manuals, which makes them easy to use but difficult to learn. Some teachers have students learn the stylebook by assigning sections weekly in alphabetic order. That approach works, but it is much like assigning students to learn a dictionary; there is too much material to be absorbed. For that reason, we have taken the most important passages from the stylebook and organized them into category groupings—capitalization, abbreviation, punctuation, numerals—in the appendix of the textbook. You can assign one of these sections each week and then use the exercises in our workbook to test students' retention of major style points. Finally, we provide stories laden with style errors to test students' skill in detecting style errors within the context of a story.

Once students have mastered the various items, you might want to test their retention of major style rules with a closed-book exam. We suggest, however, that an open-book test may be preferable. The goal should be to instill in students the habit of using the stylebook as a reference. The open-book concept reinforces that habit. There is no doubt, however, that students who are forced to memorize major style rules will benefit from the experience. No editor has the time to look up every point of style. A good working knowledge of style rules is important.

Solutions to Workbook Questions and Exercises

1. a. Lowercase "prosecuting attorney" unless this is the formal title. In most jurisdictions, the correct term is "district attorney" or "state's attorney." In some states, however, "prosecuting attorney" would be correctly capitalized. "Defense attorney" is always lowercase; it is not a formal title but is descriptive of a person's role or job.
   b. Lowercase "jeep." The military vehicle is lowercase; the civilian brand is capitalized.

c. Lowercase "legislatures." Plural forms such as these are always lowercase.

d. No errors. "War" in "Vietnam war" is lowercase because Congress never passed a formal declaration of war.

e. Lowercase "outfielder." The word is a descriptive word rather than a formal job title.

f. Capitalize "Justice Department." Government agency titles are capitalized, even when shortened from the full title (the "U.S. Department of Justice").

g. Capitalize "Mountains." The word is part of a formal title.

h. Capitalize "Latin." The names of specific ethnic or racial groups are capitalized.

i. Capitalize "Roquefort." It is a trademarked name.

j. Capitalize "FM."

2. a. Change "jeep" to "Jeep" (the commercial vehicle), unless she is buying a military jeep.

b. Change "realtor" to "Realtor," a trademarked term applied only to members of the National Association of Realtors.

c. No errors.

d. Uppercase "TV" if allowed to remain, but "television" is better.

e. Capitalize "It" because the word begins a complete quoted sentence.

f. Capitalize "Kleenex," a trademark.

g. Lowercase "secretary" and "interior."

h. Capitalize "Camel," a trademark.

i. Capitalize "God."

j. No errors.

3. a. Change "jello" to "gelatin" or "Jell-O," a trademark. Change "frigidaire" to "refrigerator" or "Frigidaire," a trademark.

b. Leave "jeep" lowercase because it refers to the army vehicle.

c. Capitalize "Coke." Change "realtor" to "real estate salesperson" or "Realtor," a trademark.

d. Lowercase "legislatures."

e. No errors.

f. Lowercase "president."

g. Lowercase "secretary of the treasury" and "administration."

h. No errors.

i. Lowercase "god."

j. No errors.

4. a. No errors.

b. Abbreviate "South" and correct the abbreviation of "Wisconsin" to "Wis."

c. Insert periods in "S.E." and abbreviate "Pennsylvania" as "Pa."

d. No errors.

e. Abbreviate "California" as "Calif."

f. Delete periods in "C.I.A."

g. Delete periods in "65 m.p.h." and "30 m.p.h."

h. Abbreviate "Wisconsin" as "Wis."

  i. Abbreviate "Wyoming" as "Wyo."
  j. No errors.

5. a. Delete "Hawaii" and commas on each side of it. Delete "Tex." and place period after "Dallas."
  b. Change "Ms." to "Miss."
  c. Change "Kans." to "Kan."
  d. Change "Apr." to "April."
  e. Change "South" to "S."
  f. Delete periods from "m.p.h."
  g. Abbreviate "January" as "Jan."
  h. Delete "Ms."
  i. Change "K.S.D.-T.V." to "KSD-TV."
  j. No errors.

6. a. Either delete comma following "it," or insert comma after first "said."
  b. Insert quotation marks around *The Grapes of Wrath,* a book title.
  c. Delete quotation marks around "TV Guide."
  d. Transpose close-quote mark and comma at end of quoted matter.
  e. No errors. Coordinating conjunction must be preceded by comma.
  f. Insert comma after "done." Another coordinating conjunction.
  g. Change comma following "Richard" to a semicolon.
  h. Hyphenate "10-year."
  i. Delete apostrophe in "1960s."

7. a. Place period inside quotation marks after "Hawaii."
  b. Delete period inside parenthesis after "John."
  c. Delete comma after "Simpson."
  d. Place comma after "1963."
  e. No errors.
  f. Make it "8- and 9-year-old girls" (suspensive hyphenation).
  g. Make it "90-yard" and "last-second."
  h. Delete hyphen after "heavily."
  i. Delete comma.
  j. Delete apostrophe in "1920s."

8. a. Change "Number One" to "No. 1."
  b. Change "3156" to "3,156."
  c. Change "fourteen" to "14."
  d. No errors.
  e. No errors.
  f. No errors.
  g. Change ".04" to "0.04."
  h. No errors.
  i. No errors.
  j. Change "3" to "three."

9. a. Make it "10-3."
  b. No errors.
  c. No errors.
  d. No errors.
  e. Make it "3 percent."

f. Change "five dollars" to "$5."

g. Change "One" to "1."

h. Change "six" to "6." You may want to insert "p.m." after "8," but it is not necessary.

i. Make it "0.04 percent."

j. No errors.

10. a. Lowercase "legislators."

b. Insert comma after "Wis.," abbreviate "South Dakota" as "S.D." and add comma afterward.

c. Insert comma after "West." (Compound sentences require commas before the coordinating conjunction.)

d. No errors.

e. Abbreviate "Brig. Gen." Lowercase "financier."

f. Capitalize "AIDS," an acronym for Acquired Immune Deficiency Syndrome.

g. Abbreviate "Del." after Wilmington.

h. Use italics for "Miami Herald" and "Herald."

i. No errors.

j. No errors.

k. Spell out "Texas."

l. Make it "24-21."

m. No errors.

n. Abbreviate "Number One" as "No. 1."

o. Hyphenate "top-rated."

p. No errors.

q. Hyphenate "most-coveted."

r. Spell out "United States." Lowercase "world."

s. No errors.

t. No errors.

u. No errors.

v. No errors.

w. No errors.

x. Place "Today" in quotation marks.

y. Insert apostrophe in "it's." Capitalize "Realtor."

11. a. The best place to eat in Rattatan, Wis., was a place called The Brat, he said, but it went out of business last year.

b. Fort Hays, Kansas, was a calvary outpost in the 1800's.

c. Brewing companies spend millions of dollars on television advertising each year, according to advertising industry experts.

d. Sergeants earn more than corporals in the U.S. army, and they earn more than lieutenants in the Russian army.

133

e. Ricardo gutierrez rode the quarterhourse to victory in the local county fair race.

f. 1984 was an election year, she told the delegates, so no texes were raised.

g. He became a first class scout in the first year he was eligible.

h. More than 4,900,000 [4.9 million] people live in that state, according to the latest figures from the United States Bureau of the census.

i. The first full year of the war 1942 was a devastating one for American morale.

j. John Wayne was an American institution for years, but he won an oscar only the last year of his life.

k. "When you go out, be sure to take the garbage," he said.

l. Its ridiculous that no boy from that school has ever been a starting quarterback at a major college considering when you the success of the program.

m. The outfieldder hit .268 in his last full seson in the majors before the leg injury halted his career.

12. A. WASHINGTON (AP)—The Treasury Department is considering restricting each American to three federally insured bank, savings institution or credit union accounts—no matter how little money is in each.

The department asked the Federal Deposit Insurance Corp. to estimate how much the proposal would save and to describe potential problems in administering it, FDIC Acting Chairman Andrew C. Hove Jr. said Wednesday.

The Independent Bankers Assn. of America is vigorously opposed.

B. WASHINGTON (AP)—The Government said home building plunged six percent in October, extending the longest construction slide on

134

record and sinking housing starts to their lowest level since the 1981-82 recession.

Industry observers pointed to shrinking consumer confidence and the growing inability of builders to obtain credit as causes of the (9-month decline reported yesterday by the Commerce Department. Many believe the slide will continue into next year.

13. At least one person is dead and six injured as a result of a two-car wreck Wednesday evening on U.S. Highway 40 west of Midway that brought out state troopers, four paramedic units and 35 Lincoln County firefighters.

Three of the injured were transported to Springfield Hospital, where one was listed in critical condition late Wednesday/ and (2) were listed in serious condition.

Three others were taken to Lincoln Hospital Center. Hospital officials refused to discuss their conditions.

One of the injured also suffered a heart attack, said Rob Brown, a Lincoln County Fire Protection District spokesperson. That person was in cardiac arrest at the scene, with no pulse or vital signs, Brown said.

Brown described the seven victims' injuries as ranging from mild back and neck problems to internal injuries. "I'm sure there were broken bones," he said.

A red Chevrolet Nova ran a stop sign at the corner of Ballard Road and Highway 40 and hit a red Ford Escort, which was moving west on Highway 40, said state trooper Charles Schaffer. Police said the intersection has a history of bad accidents.

Both cars landed in a wide ditch on the north side of the highway. The

Escort landed on its roof. Some of the passengers in both cars were thrown from the vehicles.

Police would not identify the drivers or the injured, pending notification of relatives. Witnesses said those involved in the wreck were as young as 10 years of age.

Danny Allenbaugh and Marco Arrendondo, two Fayette High School students, were among the first to arrive at the scene following the accident.

They parked their vehicle so its headlights would face both wrecked cars. The lights shone on one of the victims, a girl, who was lying in front of their car.

While they waited for ambulances to arrive, the students helped two trapped women get out of the upended Escort. The women, both students at Central Methodist College, did not seem to be seriously injured, Allenbaugh said.

14. Gusty winds fanned the flames of a Thursday afternoon fire that caused $30,000 in damage to a boardinghouse on Paris Road.

Firefighters rescued one resident from the second floor by ladder and another from the basement, said Lieutenant James Daugherty of the Springfield Fire Dept.

No one in the house at 1308 Paris Road was injured, Daugherty said, but a fireman broke a toe while working on the ladder.

At one point, all the city's major firefighting vehicles were present for the three-alarm fire, said a firefighter on the scene.

The first alarm came in at 3:32 p.m. The blaze was brought under control in fifty minutes.

Daugherty said damage to the house was mostly on the second and third floors. Careless smoking on a couch was listed as the probable cause of the fire by fire department officials.

"We've got our work cut out for us now," said R. J. Newell, owner of the house, as he stood out front surveying the damaged green and yellow building. "A lot of money there, that's what this looks like to me."

He had just finished repairing an ice machine when one of his tenants found him at work and told him the house was burning, he said. "They told me that was more important than what I was doing."

Newell, who runs a general maintenance company in Springfield, said the tenants would help him repair the damage. "They don't have any-place else to go," he said. "That's why they're here.

"Everybody will probably pitch in," Newell said. "Cooking, cleaning, building, something."

The three-story building contains 11 apartments, Newell said. (16) people were living there at the time of the fire, he said.

Several residents of the house stood across the street and watched the firefighters working. Most were worried about their possessions.

"I've got a guitar down there," said John Kendrick, who has lived in the basement for eight months.

15. A 39-year-old Springfield man was robbed early Thursday at gunpoint while making a deposit at Century State Bank, 2114 Paris Road, according to police reports.

The victim, an employee of Pizza Hut, was making a night deposit at about 1:30 A.M. when a pickup truck with two men drove into the bank parking lot.

The passenger in the pickup was wearing a mask made of a see-thru fabric similar to panty hose, said Capt. Dennis Veach of the Springfield Police Dept. The passenger got out of the truck, pulled out a hand/gun and then demanded the victim's money.

The victim handed over the cash, and the suspects drove away on Whitegate Dr.

The robbers are both white males. The driver was heavy-set and had short, dark blonde hair. The passenger was wearing blue jeans and an a jacket of unknown color jacket.

Veach said Thursday's robbery doesn't appear to be linked to two other robberies of pizza store employees in the past week. A Domino's Pizza delivery person was robbed Tuesday night at gunpoint at Ashwood Apts. 1201 Ashland Road. The victim, a 19-year-old woman, was walking back to her car at 9:30 p.m. after delivering a pizza when she was robbed.

On Dec. 27, a Domino's Pizza employee was robbed by a man with a single-barreled shotgun. That robber entered the Domino's at 3102 Green Meadows Way just before midnight.

CrimeStoppers is seeking information that could lead to the arrest of the suspects in the robberies. It is They are offering a reward and guarantees anonymity. CrimeStoppers is at 555-8477.

16. The spell of hot, dry weather that has held the area in its grasp for the last few few weeks is taking its toll on grasslands and fire fighters.

Saturday, in the wake of 15- and 25-mph winds and a high temperature of 99 degrees, fire protection agencies from across the area responded to sixteen calls.

At the largest of those, a 25-acre grass fire on Peabody Road north of Prathersville and west of Route 19, paramedics treated on sight at least five of 35 fire fighters for heat exhaustion, county fire chief Debra Schuster said.

Three more of the heavily-clad firefighters were hospitalized for heat exhaustion, and two of those were flown to Springfield Hospital by helicopter. All were treated for about 1 hour and released.

Dennis Sapp, fire captain of Station No. 1, said the blaze at Peabody Road, which burned out of control for an hour before it was contained, probably was started by a trash fire. The blaze endangered some nearby farmland and the barn on it, but was extinguished before anything but grass was burned.

Schuster said fires like the one on Peabody Road had been starting all day, especially in the northern part of the city and county. Schuster said some of the fires could have been the work of an arsonist, but careless burning was a more likely cause.

"We don't have any evidence there is an arsonist," Schuster said. "We sure hope we don't have someone running around starting fires on purpose, but there is that possibility."

COPY EDITING AND PROOFREADING SYMBOLS

1. Cole County officials will exhume the body of an elderly man to determine whether there is any connection between his death and a Springfield man arrested here on charges of first-degree robbery and of kidnapping an 85-year-old Lincoln County woman.

    Authorities said Springfield resident Eric Barnhouse, 28, an insurance salesman, may be connected to the death death of the Cole County man, the disappearance of a Troy woman, the assault of a Warrenton woman and the death of a Fulton woman. He also was charged with stealing money from an elderly Boonville woman.

    Barnhouse contacted the Cole County man just before the man's death, said Richard Lee, an investigator with the Cole County prosecuting attorney's office. Cole County officials are looking for anything that may indicate a suspicious cause of death, Lee said.

    "There was no autopsy performed at the time of death, so we're not sure what the cause of death was," Lee said.

    No charges have been filed in the Cole County case.

    Earlier this week Springfield police played host to a meeting of area law-enforcement officials interested in sharing information about Barnhouse. Since then, more charges have been filed, and Barnhouse is suspected of being involved in several other cases.

    Barnhouse was already being held in the Lincoln County Jail when Springfield police served him a Warren County warrant Jan. 9 for 1st degree burglary. Officers also charged him with resisting arrest and with probation violation from a previous Lincoln county burglary conviction.

140

Police served Barnhouse with another warrant Wednesday charging him with kidnapping and burglary of a Lincoln County woman. Barnhouse was invited into the local woman's home on ⬭December⬭ 31 after he identified himself as an insurance agent, police said.

According to police, Barnhouse returned to the woman's home later that day and asked her for a check for ⓑ insurance premiums. The woman refused, and he held her at gunpoint and demanded she go to the bank and cash a check.

After driving around Springfield for several hours with the victim, the woman gave Barnhouse $60, and he returned her to her home unharmed.

When Springfield police arrested Barnhouse on Jan. 9, they discovered the purse of a woman who disappeared the same day from her home in Troy, which is 50 miles northwest of St. Louis.

Springfield police also believe Barnhouse posed as an insurance agent Jan. 7 to an 84-year-old woman in Warrenton.

According to the victim's statement, she was beaten unconscious. He had placed a rag with some type of liquid over her mouth before she passed out, she said.

Fulton police are waiting for a toxicologist's report on the death of an elderly woman they believe Barnhouse called on before she died. Barnhouse attempted to cash a check from the woman's account, said Mick Herbert, Fulton Police Chief. Results of her autopsy were inconclusive.

2.   Springfield police have arrested a local woman three times in the past ⑨ months, most recently on Thursday in connection with the December attempted robbery of a taxi driver.

Willa Walter, 34, of 3601 W. Ash Street was arrested by Springfield police at 2:52 a.m. Thursday. Police "had not even considered her as a suspect" before receiving a Crimestoppers tip Wednesday, Capt. Dennis Veach said. Walter remained in the Lincoln County Jail on Thursday afternoon in lieu of $25,000 bail.

Police arrested Walter for the Dec. 14 attempted robbery of a Bob's Checker Cab. The taxi driver had delivered a woman to the intersection of Garth Ave. and Sexton Rd, Veach said, when she pulled out a revolver and demanded money. After a brief struggle, the woman fled without the cash. At the time of the incident, Walter was free on bond from another armed robbery arrest, this one involving the April 9 holdup of a Texaco gas station at 2102 W. Ash St. Springfield police arrested her a few hours after the robbery, thanks to a witness at the gas station who wrote down her car's license plate number. She pleaded guilty Nov. 30.

But Walter and the police met again fairly soon. Less than a month later, Walter was arrested again, this time on misdemeanor theft, assault and marijuana possession charges. She awaits sentencing for those charges Feb. 25.

3. A Crime Stopper call helped police find a suspect in the Tuesday shooting of a 28-year- old Springfield man.

Police arrested Aaron Brewster, 24, of St. Balentine on Friday at about 10 a.m.

Police received a call about a shooting on Allen Walkway about 9:55 p.m. Tuesday. They arrived and found a man on the ground with a single gunshot wound just above the heart, said Cpt. Chris Egbert of the Springfield Police Department.

Following surgery, the victim was in stable condition at Lincoln County Hospital on Friday. Police did not know his condition Saturday.

Brewster had been staying in Springfield for a few months but calls St. Balentine his home, said Sgt. Bill Haws.

The shooting, which occurred near the victims house, was the result of an argument about a female friend of the two men. Several people were present, including the woman over whom they were arguing, Haws said.

Police arrested Brewster without incident at 908 North Garth Ave.

Brewster remained in the Lincoln County Jail on Saturday on charges of probation and parole violation, armed criminal action and first-degree assault. Bond has not been set.

4.   Springfield police arrested a local woman on suspicion of forging and cashing bogus payroll checks at area supermarkets.

Shirley M. Hannah of 1301 Ridge Road was released from Lincoln County Jail after posting a $45,000 bond, a sheriff's department spokesperson said.

Hayes, 21 was arrested Saturday after an employee of Food Barn, 705 Business Loop 70 West, recognized her because she'd previously bounced a check at the store, Sgt. Dean France said.

France said investigators believe Hannah was working with at least one other person for about a week. Capt. Mick Covington said they opened a fake business account at a Springfield bank to obtain bogus payroll checks.

"It appears someone opened a fraudulent account in the same name as a legitimate company, France said. He said Hannah is suspected of cashing at least twelve checks.